# kid chef
# Vegan

# kid chef Vegan

*The* FOODIE KID'S VEGAN COOKBOOK

Barb Musick

ROCKRIDGE
PRESS

For general information on our other products and services or to obtain technical support, please contact our Customer Care Department within the United States at (866) 744-2665, or outside the United States at (510) 253-0500.

Rockridge Press publishes its books in a variety of electronic and print formats. Some content that appears in print may not be available in electronic books, and vice versa.

Interior and Cover Designer: Gabe Nansen
Art Producer: Sara Feinstein
Editor: Marjorie DeWitt

Photography © 2021 Emulsion Studio, cover; Annie Martin, p. ii, vi, viii, 11, 20, 24, 28, 32, 36, 40, 44, 50, 53-54, 58, 60, 68, 74, 84, 94, 102, 114, 116, 118, 122, 127, 128, 134; Evi Abeler, pps. x-1, 12, 139; Darren Muir, p. 2, 34-35; Marija Vidal, p. 49, 136-137; Tara Donne, p. 101. Author photo courtesy of Angela Prodanova.

ISBN: Print 978-1-63807-415-1
    eBook 978-1-63807-244-7
R0

FOR THE ANIMALS.

# CONTENTS

Cherry-Berry Smoothies (page 17)

# INTRODUCTION

**Hello, and welcome to this vegan cooking adventure!** My name is Barb, and I love creating delicious vegan meals for my friends and family. For me, spending time in the kitchen is a lot of fun, and sharing the food I make is a great way to show my love and appreciation for those I care about.

I didn't always know how to cook. When I was a kid, I only had one recipe, for apple pie, and it was all I ever made. I made it so often, I learned the recipe by heart! My hope is that you will be much more adventurous in the kitchen than I was. As you spend more time honing your skills and exploring new types of ingredients and dishes from around the world, you'll learn what flavors and textures you like best. Then you can continue experimenting and growing as a home cook!

Whether you're new to cooking or have been practicing a lot, I think you'll find this book very helpful in your journey. I've included a lot of information in the second chapter to help you learn and practice new skills. They are set up as lessons, and each one includes a recipe tutorial so you can practice the new skill you just learned.

If getting in the kitchen and creating delicious meals sounds like it will be hard, don't worry. We start with the basics and go from there. No matter where you are in your cooking journey, there are recipes in this book just for you!

Speaking of the recipes . . . they are all in part 2 of this book, and each one has easy-to-follow instructions. They also have tips that will teach you fun facts about the ingredients or give you ideas on how to change the recipe and make it unique. Best of all, the recipes are all delicious, and I hope you enjoy them!

# PART ONE
# Cooking Skills

Welcome to part 1 of this cookbook, where I share the tools and appliances that I use the most (and that are referred to in the recipes here in this book), along with kitchen safety tips. I've also shared some common cooking skills that are important for all home cooks to know and even cooking tutorials!

# 1

# Your Plant-Based Kitchen

Whether you're new to cooking or have been helping in the kitchen for a long time, there is always more to learn and new tools, techniques, and ingredients to try. This chapter provides an overview of the basics you'll need to tackle the recipes in this book, including tools, plant-based ingredients and alternatives, and safety tips. I want you to have fun in the kitchen and make lots of delicious food for your family and friends, so let's get started!

# GO-TO GUIDELINES

Cooking and baking can be a lot of fun, but they can quickly become not so fun if your food doesn't turn out right, you hurt yourself, or you are left with a giant pile of dirty pots, pans, and dishes when you're done. Follow these basic kitchen rules, and you'll be on your way to delicious results:

**Check the details.** Before you start cooking or baking, read the recipe from beginning to end. Make sure you understand the steps and have all the ingredients and equipment on hand.

**Grab an adult.** Most recipes in this book require some knifework and/or the stovetop or oven, so it's important to have an adult nearby to assist you.

**Safety first.** Although cross-contamination is less of a risk with vegan ingredients (because you aren't handling raw chicken, for example), food safety is still important! Nondairy milk, butter, and yogurt need to be kept refrigerated. You also need to watch out for sharp knives and hot pans (keep reading for more on stove and oven safety).

**Prep the area.** Clean your workspace and set up your ingredients and tools before you start a new recipe. This means double-checking that you have all the equipment (and ingredients!) you'll need (cutting board, knives, mixing bowls, measuring spoons, etc.), and prewashing any fruits or veggies you'll be cutting.

**Prep the cook.** The cook needs to be prepped, too! Make sure your hands are washed and that you have an apron or clean hand towels nearby. I like to tie my hair back so it doesn't distract me (or get in the food!).

**Clean as you go.** I am a big fan of cleaning as I cook, as are many pro chefs. When you wash your dishes and tools as soon as you're done with them, it keeps your workspace clean and organized (you're less likely to misplace a tool or skip an ingredient) and reduces the amount of cleanup work you'll have to do when you're done cooking.

# IS IT VEGAN?

It can be easy to get *vegan* and *vegetarian* confused, especially if the words are new to you. Vegetarian foods aren't meat or anything that has meat in it. Vegan foods don't have meat in them, and they also do not contain eggs or dairy (like yogurt or ice cream made with cow's milk). Think of it like this: Everything that is vegan is also vegetarian, but not everything that is vegetarian is also vegan. Here's a helpful chart to help you understand.

| | VEGAN | VEGETARIAN |
|---|---|---|
| EGGS | | X |
| DAIRY MILK AND CHEESE | | X |
| TOFU | X | X |
| TEMPEH | X | X |
| MILK MADE FROM NUTS, COCONUT, OR OATS | X | X |
| ICE CREAM MADE FROM NUTS, COCONUT, OR OATS | X | X |
| BEANS | X | X |
| LENTILS | X | X |
| VEGETABLE BROTH OR STOCK | X | X |
| WHOLE GRAINS LIKE RICE | X | X |

# HANDY KITCHEN TOOLS

Successful chefs have good tools, and here is an overview of some of the equipment you'll need for the recipes in this book. There's no need to go out and stock up all at once, though! Make do with what you (or your household) already have and build your collection as you continue to grow as a home chef.

## Cookware & Bakeware

 **Baking dish:** Usually glass or ceramic and rectangular in shape, this can be used for making everything from casseroles to baked pasta dishes.

 **Colander:** This is the funny-looking bowl with holes in it. It drains water from cooked pasta and vegetables so you don't burn yourself.

 **Large pot with a lid:** A very important tool, this pot is used for boiling water, making soups and sauces, and making recipes that are too large to fit in a skillet.

 **Sheet pan:** This is a metal rectangular pan with a small lip around the edge. It's used for baking cookies and bar-type desserts, as well as for roasting vegetables and baking things like tofu.

 **Skillet:** Also called a frying pan, this flat-bottomed pan with a handle is used mostly for frying and browning, but it can also be used for other kinds of cooking.

## Tools & Utensils

 **Knives:** Having at least one good chopping knife is important, and having a few different types is even better. There are many kinds of knives, but the most important are a chef's knife for cutting and chopping, a serrated bread knife for slicing bread without tearing it, and a paring knife for peeling, slicing, and removing seeds from fruits and vegetables.

**Measuring cups and spoons:** Make sure you have a liquid measuring cup (this will likely be glass or plastic with a handle, spout, and measuring lines on the side), a set of dry measuring cups (likely metal or plastic), and a set of measuring spoons. You can't measure ingredients properly without these items!

 **Peeler:** There are different styles of peelers, and any will work to remove the tough skin from vegetables like potatoes and squash.

 **Spatulas:** These tools come in all different shapes and sizes, but the two most important are rubber (or silicone) scraping spatulas and flat turning spatulas. Flat spatulas are used for flipping things in a pan (like pancakes) and for moving food from a dish to a plate. Rubber or silicone spatulas are great for mixing wet and sticky ingredients, since they are designed to scrape the sides of bowls or pots.

 **Tongs:** You'll want a pair of tongs for picking food out of boiling water or off a hot tray. They can seem tricky to use at first, but you'll get the hang of it before you know it.

## Small Appliances

 **Blender:** This is used to mix and puree foods. It can be stationary, sitting on your counter, or a "stick" or immersion blender that you dip into your pot or mixing bowl.

 **Electric mixer:** Most commonly used in baking recipes, this helps you mix wet and dry ingredients quickly and easily. A larger stand mixer works equally well for the recipes in this book, if you have one.

 **Food processor:** One of my favorite tools! You can use it to blend, chop, dice, and grate fruits, nuts, cheeses, and veggies.

 **Tofu press:** This tool allows you to easily and neatly remove the excess liquid from tofu, allowing you to control the texture of your tofu (the drier it is, the chewier and "meatier" it'll be). Learn more about this on page 23.

# TOP KITCHEN SAFETY TIPS

1. Keep pan handles turned toward the back of the stove so they don't stick out over the edge. This helps prevent accidentally bumping into them, which can cause spilled food and burns!

2. Always use an oven mitt or pot holder when handling hot pots and pans, but don't let it get wet. A wet pot holder will not protect your hands from burns.

3. Don't wear loose clothing, and always tie back long hair.

4. Wipe up spills immediately, especially those on the floor that you could slip on while cooking.

5. Keep a fire extinguisher in the kitchen or nearby.

6. Never leave the kitchen when you have something cooking on the stovetop.

7. Never leave the house when you have something baking in the oven.

8. Always be sure the blender or food processor is unplugged before attempting to remove the blades.

9. Always be careful and keep your face back when removing lids from hot foods, since the steam can burn your skin.

10. Hold knives by their handles only, and always be careful with the blades.

11. Always be careful when opening canned goods. The inner edge of the lid can be very sharp (ask an adult to help if needed).

# STOCK UP

Let's talk ingredients! Here are some go-to plant-based foods and seasonings every kitchen should have.

## Pantry

These shelf-stable (meaning they don't need to be refrigerated) staples are always useful to have at the ready.

**Canned beans:** When you have a few different types of canned beans on hand, you can create all sorts of healthy, satisfying meals in no time.

**Good-quality oils:** I prefer avocado and olive oils, along with a general vegetable oil, which is good for when you don't want a strong flavor.

**Kala namak salt:** Also called "black salt," this seasoning gives you the secret power to make anything taste like eggs! You'll see it in all my "eggy" breakfast dishes, like Breakfast Tacos (page 45) and Egg-Like Tofu Breakfast Sandwiches (page 48).

**Nonstick cooking spray:** This helps keep food from sticking to pots and pans, especially when baking.

**Nutritional yeast:** This is such a popular ingredient that it has a nickname: "nooch." It has a nice cheesy flavor. You can sprinkle it onto tofu or into sauces or even use it to make vegan "cheesy" popcorn.

**Seasoned salt:** There are many types of seasoned salt to choose from, but I like the Italian version because it can be used on just about any vegetable.

**Smoked paprika:** Not to be confused with regular paprika, this version has a smoky, almost bacon-like flavor.

## Refrigerator & Freezer

These are the most useful ingredients to keep in your refrigerator and freezer for everyday vegan meals.

**Frozen vegetables:** Frozen vegetables are versatile and inexpensive; plus, they can be added to any recipe you want to "bulk up."

**Nondairy milk:** There are many kinds of nondairy milk. Once you find your favorite, keep it on hand for cereal, smoothies, and even sauces and baked treats. My favorite is unsweetened cashew milk!

**Real maple syrup:** It's not just for pancakes! Maple syrup works as a sweetener in all sorts of dishes—just be sure to get real (a.k.a. pure maple) syrup, not the imitation "pancake syrup." The real stuff is less processed, so it's healthier and tastes much better!

**Tempeh:** Using this vegan protein is a very easy way to add "meaty" texture to a recipe, and you can even make plant-based bacon, like Baked Tempeh Bacon (page 47) out of it.

**Tofu (firm or extra-firm):** Tofu is a protein made of soy that is easy to flavor and can be cooked in lots of ways.

**Vegan butter:** You can buy this in sticks or tubs (just like regular butter), and it's good to keep some of both on hand for baking and cooking.

**Vegan cheese:** Just like with nondairy milk, try the different options and find your favorite brand. Most of the recipes in the book use naturally vegan foods, but vegan cheese can be a fun option every once in a while.

# 2

# Vegan Cooking Skills

This chapter will help you establish and improve your cooking skills. You'll learn how to read and understand a recipe and all about knife safety and cutting techniques. I even share one of the most important things a vegan home cook needs to know: how to press tofu! The lessons include recipes so you can practice the skills as you learn them, too. Whether you are just starting off in the kitchen or already have had a lot of practice, it is always good to perfect your basic skills.

# THE VERY BASICS

When it comes to cooking, it's important to start with the basics. In fact, even the most successful chefs in the world first had to learn how to read a recipe and measure their ingredients before they could move on to learning more advanced skills.

## Reading a Recipe

One of the most important things a good home cook does is read the recipe from beginning to end *before* they start cooking! In fact, I recommend reading the recipe twice to make sure you understand all the individual steps and the overall process. This helps ensure that you have all the ingredients and tools you need. I've jumped into recipes without reading them all the way through before, only to end up realizing halfway that I'm missing an ingredient. It's not fun!

**Recipe titles:** The name of a recipe will often give you a good idea of the type of dish and flavors you can expect, and it's often the thing that pulls you in and inspires you to make it!

**Yield:** This is usually how many servings a recipe makes, although sometimes you'll also see it as a yield in size (such as cups).

**Ingredients:** This is an important list! Read through all the ingredients, then lay them out on the counter. This will help ensure you have everything you need and stay organized. Also note how ingredients are described to know if you need to prepare them before you start cooking. For example, if the recipe calls for "1 can black beans," then all you need is that can of beans. Or it might read "1 can black beans, drained and rinsed" which means you should prep that ingredient before moving on to the next steps.

**Tools/equipment needed:** This is a list of all the kitchen tools you'll need to make this recipe. I recommend gathering them all before you get started, just like you did with the ingredients.

**Directions:** Now we get to the fun part, where you start creating! The recipes in this book are very detailed, and it is important to follow them precisely. If you skip a step or try to do them out of order, it's very possible that the dish won't turn out the way it was meant to. Don't forget to clean up as you go, and always, if you're unsure of what something means, ask an adult.

# Measuring Ingredients

Measuring is very important because if you don't start with the right amount of each ingredient, the recipe won't work—you'll wind up with textures that are too mushy or too crunchy or flavors that are all wrong. Here are some tips for proper measuring.

**Wet ingredients:** When measuring wet or liquid ingredients, be sure to use the liquid measuring cup (the one with a handle and spout). The lines for measuring (½ cup, 1 cup, etc.) are printed on the side. Place the measuring cup on the counter and pour the liquid into it until you get to the desired measurement line. Placing the cup on the counter keeps it steady and allows for precise measuring. For small amounts of liquid, use measuring spoons.

**Dry ingredients:** For dry ingredients such as flour, sugar, and oats or grains, use the measuring cups that are individually identified by their exact amount (¼ cup, ½ cup, etc.), and that often are scoop- or cup-shaped. Unless the recipe calls for the ingredient to be "packed" (this is most common with brown sugar), you should never try to compress it in the cup. You should also use a straight edge, like the back of a table knife, to scrape along the top to make sure the measuring cup is full but level, with no extra mounding on top. The same goes for measuring spoons; you don't want the ingredients to be rounded at the top.

**Other ingredients:** What about ingredients that aren't exactly dry or liquid, like almond butter or coconut oil? For small amounts of these ingredients, use measuring spoons and an additional spoon or butter knife to help scrape the sticky butter or oil into your mixing bowl. For larger amounts, use your dry measuring cups, along with a butter knife or scraper to make sure it all ends up in the mixing bowl or pan.

# VEGAN GROCERY SHOPPING

I have found that the key to a successful and enjoyable trip to the grocery store is *being organized*. What does this mean? Well, it can be different for each family, but to me it means knowing what you want and where to find it. Once you figure out what works best for you and your family, I think you'll find grocery shopping enjoyable, too! Here are some tips to get you started.

1. **Start with what you have on hand.** When I'm planning my meals for the week, I always start by taking a look in the pantry and refrigerator to see what I already have on hand. This will help keep you from buying ingredients you already have.

2. **Make a list.** Even if you're only buying one or two items, always bring a list with you. Trust me, it's easy to get distracted and forget what you went for.

3. **Get to know your grocery store.** After a few visits, you'll learn the layout of the store, and that will help you with your list. You can start to organize it by sections (produce, pasta, dairy alternatives, etc.), which will help make your trip faster.

4. **Learn your ingredients.** The more you cook, the more familiar you'll become with the ingredients. This is especially helpful with fruits and veggies and being able to tell if they're fresh and ripe.

5. **Think on your feet!** Sometimes the store will be out of the ingredient you need, and you'll have to make a decision on how to substitute. As you get more comfortable, you'll learn which ingredients make the best substitutes for one another (like sweet potatoes and butternut squash!).

6. **Don't be afraid to try new things.** Whether it's a last-minute substitution or a planned purchase, don't be afraid to try new foods! You just might find your new favorite flavor that way.

# Cherry-Berry Smoothies

**PREP TIME:** 10 MINUTES

**SERVES:** 2

2 small or medium bananas,
  peeled and broken in half
12 frozen pitted cherries
1 cup fresh blueberries
1 cup unsweetened nondairy milk
1 cup ice cubes (doesn't need to
  be exact)

**TOOLS/EQUIPMENT**

- Blender
- Measuring cups and spoons

**Combine the ingredients.**

Put the bananas, cherries, blueberries, milk, and ice cubes in a blender. Close and secure the lid.

**Blend.**

Plug in and turn on the blender. Pulse or process on low speed for 15 to 20 seconds, or until no more ice chunks remain. If you want to check, unplug the blender, remove the cover, and use a spoon to fish around for any pieces of ice. Pour the smoothie into 2 glasses and enjoy.

TROUBLESHOOTING: Smoothie not sweet enough? It could be that the blueberries weren't quite ripe. Try tasting a berry before blending, and if you need to, add 1 tablespoon agave syrup to the blender.

# CUTTING TECHNIQUES

It's good to be familiar with cutting techniques, and you'll find that your skills improve over time. Here are five of the most common cuts you'll find called for in recipes.

**Chop.** Cut the ingredient into bite-size pieces about the size of a nickel. "Finely chopped" means the food is cut into pieces smaller than bite-size, yet still larger than diced.

**Dice.** Cut food into small, square pieces that are still large enough to be identified.

**Mince.** Cut food into tiny pieces. This cut often requires taking a second or third pass with your knife. If there is a large amount of food that needs to be minced, it can be quicker and easier to use a food processor.

**Slice.** Hold the piece of food firmly on a cutting board with one hand (fingers curled back and under) and then, with the other hand, use a knife to cut straight down through the food, or use a sawing motion to make thin slices (the shape will depend on the food you are slicing).

**Halve.** This means to cut the ingredient in two equal halves. Depending on the ingredient you're working with, it may also include removing a seed, such as with an avocado.

# KNIFE SAFETY TIPS

**Keep a steady grip.** It's important to have a firm, steady grip on the handle of the knife. This gives you more control while you're chopping and slicing and helps ensure that the knife doesn't accidentally slip or drop.

**Watch your fingers.** While one hand is holding the knife, the other hand will be holding the ingredients. You should always curl your fingers back in and under when holding ingredients to be chopped, almost like making a claw.

**Never hold a knife by the blade.** Always hold the knife by the handle and keep the blade pointed down (and away from anyone else in the kitchen with you).

**Never fool around with knives.** Being in the kitchen should be fun, but knives are serious business! Always stay focused on what you're doing when knives are involved.

**Keep your knives sharp.** Dull blades are the most likely to slip while you're slicing fruits and veggies, so they are very dangerous. Ask your adult helper about having your knife blades sharpened.

Fruity Spinach Salad

# Fruity Spinach Salad

**PREP TIME:** 20 MINUTES

**SERVES:** 4

1 cup fresh strawberries

1 cup fresh blueberries

1 cup fresh blackberries

6 cups fresh baby spinach

½ cup chopped walnuts

¼ teaspoon salt

⅛ teaspoon freshly ground
    black pepper

¼ cup balsamic salad dressing,
    plus more for serving

**TOOLS/EQUIPMENT**

- Cutting board
- Knife
- Measuring cups and spoons
- Large mixing bowl
- Spoon

**Slice the strawberries.**

Cut off the strawberries' leafy tops and throw them away. Cut the strawberries into slices.

**Mix the salad.**

In a large mixing bowl, combine the sliced strawberries, blueberries, blackberries, spinach, walnuts, salt, and pepper. Mix well.

**Add the dressing.**

Drizzle on the salad dressing, then mix again until everything is coated. Serve the salad with extra dressing on the side.

PRO TIP: To make a homemade balsamic vinaigrette: In a Mason jar or other container with a tightly closing lid, combine 1½ cups extra-virgin olive oil, ½ cup balsamic vinegar, 3 tablespoons real maple syrup, 1 teaspoon Dijon mustard, 1 teaspoon garlic powder, 1 teaspoon salt, and 1 teaspoon freshly ground black pepper. Seal the lid and shake as hard as you can until the ingredients are combined and smooth. This makes 2 cups. Leftovers will stay fresh in a refrigerated air-tight container for up to 1 week.

TRY INSTEAD: To make this salad a bit more filling, stir in 1 cup cooked quinoa before tossing with the dressing.

# ESSENTIAL PREP

In addition to cutting and measuring, there are additional skills every home chef should have, no matter their age. Here are just a few that I think you will find helpful.

**Folding.** Gently adding an ingredient to your mixture by using a spoon or spatula to scoop the mixture up from the bottom of the bowl and over the new ingredient just until that ingredient is incorporated.

**Grating.** Shredding an ingredient into much smaller pieces. This can be done with a box grater, food processor, or handheld zester.

**Mixing.** Combining multiple ingredients, usually in a bowl with a spoon or maybe in a blender or food processor. It's important to make sure everything is completely mixed and you don't see any chunks of an ingredient left (unless it says otherwise in the recipe).

**Peeling.** Removing the skin from a fruit or veggie, usually with a peeler tool.

# PRESSING TOFU

When it comes to mastering the art of plant-based cooking, learning how to press tofu is just as important as learning how to properly measure and chop vegetables and other ingredients. Why? Because to get flavor *into* your tofu, you first have to get the water *out*. You'll notice that the recipes in this book that use tofu call for it to be "well pressed." There are two main ways of doing this.

## DO IT YOURSELF.

You can press tofu with items you have around the house. Start by cutting the tofu into smaller, thinner slices as called for in the recipe (or just cut it once through the middle, creating two thinner rectangles). Use a paper towel to pat the tofu dry. Place a clean, folded kitchen towel on a cutting board, then put a double layer of paper towels on top. Arrange the tofu pieces in a single layer on the paper towels, then top with another double layer of paper towels and another clean kitchen towel. Top with a second cutting board. If you like, you can carefully place a book or other heavy item on top of the second cutting board—just be careful not to add anything too heavy or the tofu will get smashed, not pressed. Let the tofu press for 30 minutes to 1 hour, changing the paper towels and kitchen towels if they get soaked.

## USE A TOFU PRESS.

For less than $30, you (or your adult helper) can buy a tofu press online that will make it easy to squeeze unwanted liquid from a block of tofu in minutes. This allows you, then, to add the flavor you want to the tofu, either with a marinade or by allowing the tofu to soak up a sauce while cooking. There are different brands, materials, and price points to choose from.

Mixed Veggie and Hummus Wraps

# Mixed Veggie and Hummus Wraps

**PREP TIME:** 15 MINUTES

**SERVES:** 4

1 carrot

1 celery stalk

1 cup broccoli florets

1 (10-ounce) container plain hummus

4 individual pitas, or 2 large round pitas, halved

Optional toppings: Lettuce, sliced tomato, sliced avocado, sliced vegan cheese of choice

**TOOLS/EQUIPMENT**

- Peeler
- Cutting board
- Knife
- Food processor
- Medium mixing bowl
- Spoon

**Prepare the veggies.**

Peel the carrot. Chop the carrot and celery into about 1-inch pieces. Put the carrot, celery, and broccoli in a food processor. Pulse for 6 to 8 seconds, or until the vegetables are in very small pieces.

**Mix the spread and build the wraps.**

Transfer the vegetable pieces to a medium mixing bowl. Stir in the hummus. Spoon one-fourth of the mixture into each pita and add any desired toppings.

MIX IT UP: Any crunchy vegetables you have on hand will work in this wrap. Cauliflower, bell pepper, and cucumber would all be yummy additions.

PRO TIP: Take this wrap up a notch by using a flavored or spicy hummus. Grocery stores carry a wide variety of flavors, many of which would go well with fresh, crisp veggies.

# ON THE STOVETOP

Whether you are more of a cook or a baker, you'll need to be comfortable using a stovetop. In fact, I use my stovetop much more than I use my oven, and you very well might, too.

**Gas stove versus electric stove.** A lot of cooking is done on the stovetop, so it's important to know how to use this appliance safely. Induction and most electric stovetops have smooth, flat surfaces. Some may glow red as a warning when they're hot. Gas stovetops have grates with an open flame when turned on.

**Simmering and boiling.** Simmering is when the liquid is just below boiling, and there are fewer and slower bubbles. This is usually done using low or medium-low heat. Boiling is when the liquid is bubbling furiously and turning into steam. This is almost always done at high heat.

**Sautéing, stir-frying.** Sautéing and stir-frying mean to fry quickly, usually in oil (but it can also be done in water or broth) and would be done over medium-high or high heat.

**Grilling.** Grilling on the stovetop requires a special pan and can be done over any temperature setting, depending on what you are grilling (so follow the recipe!).

**Stove safety.** You need to be extra careful to keep towels (and your shirtsleeves!) away from the flames. If you're not sure which type of stovetop you have, ask an adult, and always be sure to follow the house rules when using it.

# VEGAN SUBSTITUTIONS

There are so many easy-to-find plant-based substitutes for cooks and bakers today! Here's what to reach for whenever you're craving a non-vegan food.

| USE THIS | INSTEAD OF THIS |
| --- | --- |
| ALMOND, CASHEW, COCONUT, OR SOY MILK | DAIRY MILK |
| CRUMBLED TOFU OR SOAKED CASHEWS | RICOTTA |
| STORE-BOUGHT BRANDS LIKE FOLLOW YOUR HEART, CHAO CREAMERY BY FIELD ROAST, AND DAIYA | SLICED AND SHREDDED CHEESE |
| TOFU SEASONED WITH KALA NAMAK SALT | SCRAMBLED EGGS |
| ¼ CUP UNSWEETENED APPLESAUCE | 1 EGG (IN BAKING) |
| 1 BANANA, SMASHED | 1 EGG (IN BAKING) |
| STORE-BOUGHT EGG SUBSTITUTES LIKE FOLLOW YOUR HEART VEGANEGG AND JUST EGG | EGGS IN COOKING AND BAKING |
| STORE-BOUGHT VEGAN MAYONNAISE, YOGURT, AND BUTTER | STANDARD MAYONNAISE, YOGURT, AND BUTTER |
| REAL MAPLE SYRUP | HONEY |

Easy 3-Bean Chili

# Easy 3-Bean Chili

**PREP TIME:** 10 MINUTES

**COOK TIME:** 25 MINUTES

**SERVES:** 6

1 (15-ounce) can red kidney beans

1 (15-ounce) can black beans

1 (15-ounce) can pinto beans

1 (15-ounce) can diced tomatoes

1 cup frozen corn

1½ teaspoons dried oregano

1 teaspoon ground cumin

1 teaspoon smoked paprika

¾ teaspoon salt, plus more
for seasoning

½ teaspoon chili powder, plus
more for seasoning

½ teaspoon onion powder

⅛ teaspoon kala namak salt

3 cups vegetable broth

Optional toppings: Sliced avocado,
crushed tortilla chips, shredded
vegan cheese of choice

**TOOLS/EQUIPMENT**

- Can opener
- Colander
- Measuring cups and spoons
- Large stockpot with lid

**Mix the ingredients.**

Drain and rinse the kidney beans, black beans, and pinto beans. Put them in a large stockpot. Add the tomatoes with their juices, corn, oregano, cumin, paprika, salt, chili powder, onion powder, kala namak salt, and vegetable broth. Stir well.

**Let the chili simmer.**

Bring the chili to a simmer over medium heat. Reduce the heat to low. Cover the pot and cook, stirring occasionally, for 20 minutes. Remove from the heat.

**Season and serve.**

Taste, adding more salt, chili powder, or both if desired. Serve with optional toppings as you like.

PRO TIP: Want spicier chili? Choose diced tomatoes with green chiles, or try adding red pepper flakes along with the other spices in step 1. Start with just a pinch and work your way up.

DID YOU KNOW? Chili is almost always better the second day, after the flavors have had time to meld together. Consider making this chili ahead or making extra so you have leftovers!

# IN THE OVEN

If you love to bake, the oven is your best friend. Getting to know your oven is an important first step whether you're making a cake, cookies, or a pie.

**Oven safety.** Before starting a recipe using the oven, peek inside to make sure there are no baking sheets, pans, or other items in there. If the recipe calls for a certain rack position, now is also the time to adjust it (before the oven is hot). If the recipe doesn't specify a certain rack, use the center one. Once the oven is hot, be mindful when opening the door. You need to be careful not to burn yourself on the inside edges of the oven door, and you also don't want anyone else in the kitchen to bump into it. Finally, it's always a good idea to keep oven mitts handy and remember that the oven can take a long time to cool down after you've turned it off.

**Preheating and temperature.** Preheating the oven is important, and most recipes call for you to do that as your very first step. This gives the oven time to heat up while you put together the recipe, so that it's ready when you are.

**Baking and roasting.** Baking and roasting are methods that cook food in the oven with dry heat without an open flame.

**Broiling.** This is when you cook something by placing it very close to the radiant heat source on the top inside of your oven. It's often used for short periods of time to brown the top of a dish.

**How to know when it's done.** This depends on what you are making. Follow the recipe for signs that your dish has finished cooking. For example, the rice or pasta should be tender or the potatoes browned on top.

# FREQUENTLY ASKED VEGAN QUESTIONS

Here are answers to some questions and problems that might come up as you learn how to cook for yourself and your family.

### DO I HAVE TO ADD THE INGREDIENTS IN A SPECIFIC ORDER? WHAT HAPPENS IF I DON'T?

**Most recipes need to be followed the way they're written.** This is especially true in baking, where not following the recipe could ruin the dish. In cooking, not following the recipe can change the flavor or change the dish altogether.

### HOW DO WE KNOW WHICH INGREDIENTS AND FLAVORS GO WELL TOGETHER?

**Some combinations are well known (like peanut butter and chocolate, or tomatoes and basil), but others may be discovered by experimenting.**

### WHAT IF I DON'T LIKE THE FRUIT OR VEGETABLE IN A RECIPE?

**Swap it out for something you like more.** Use the same amount of the new ingredient and cut it to the same size indicated for the ingredient you're swapping out. For example, if you don't like the peas called for in the Veggie Pasta Salad (page 77), add more diced bell pepper, some broccoli florets, or whatever other vegetables you like!

### WHAT DOES "SEASON TO TASTE" MEAN?

**Some people like their food spicier or saltier or sweeter than others, so the recipes in this book keep ingredients like salt, sugar, and hot spices and sauces to a minimum.** This means it's up to you if you want to add more. You should always add a little at a time, though, because once it's in there, you can't take it out!

### DO I REALLY NEED TO PRESS THE TOFU?

**Yes.** If you don't remove the excess water the tofu comes packed in, the tofu will be soft and mushy. See the instructions for pressing tofu on page 23. The exception to this is tofu you buy already seasoned and baked.

Sweet 'n' Spicy
Crispy Roasted Chickpeas

# Sweet 'n' Spicy Crispy Roasted Chickpeas

**PREP TIME:** 10 MINUTES
**COOK TIME:** 30 MINUTES
**SERVES:** 4

Nonstick cooking spray, for
  coating the baking sheet
2 (15-ounce) cans chickpeas
1 tablespoon plus 2 teaspoons
  packed light brown sugar
½ teaspoon garlic powder
½ teaspoon chili powder
½ teaspoon salt
½ teaspoon ground cumin
¼ teaspoon paprika
⅛ teaspoon freshly ground
  black pepper
1 tablespoon avocado oil or
  olive oil

**TOOLS/EQUIPMENT**

- Large rimmed baking sheet
- Can opener
- Colander
- Clean kitchen towel
- Small mixing bowl
- Measuring cups and spoons
- Spoon
- Oven mitts or pot holders

**Turn on the oven and prep your baking sheet.**
Preheat the oven to 420°F. Lightly coat a large rimmed baking sheet with cooking spray.

**Cook the chickpeas.**
Drain and rinse the chickpeas, then pat dry using a clean towel. Spread them in a single layer on the prepared baking sheet. Transfer them to the oven and bake for 15 minutes.

**Mix the seasoning.**
While the chickpeas bake, in a small mixing bowl, stir together the brown sugar, garlic powder, chili powder, salt, cumin, paprika, and pepper.

**Dress the chickpeas.**
Using oven mitts, remove the baking sheet from the oven, leaving the oven on. Place the baking sheet on a trivet or large pot holder. Drizzle the avocado oil over the chickpeas, then sprinkle on the seasoning. Give the chickpeas a good stir, and using oven mitts again, put the baking sheet back in the oven for 10 to 15 minutes, or until the chickpeas are nice and crispy. Using oven mitts again, remove the chickpeas from the oven. Let cool before snacking.

DID YOU KNOW? These make for a great snack for when you're on the go! After they've cooled, try packing them in individual-serving size containers that you can grab on your way out the door.

# PART TWO
# Recipes

And now, what we've all been waiting for: the recipes.
I really channeled my inner teenager while writing
this book, and I think these are recipes that you
will enjoy both making and eating. I focused on
creating delicious flavors with simple techniques to
make vegan cooking easy and enjoyable no matter
how comfortable you are in the kitchen. Enjoy!

Baked Tempeh Bacon (page 47)

# 3

# Breakfast & Brunch

# Cinnamon Swirl Pancakes

PREP TIME: 20 MINUTES
COOK TIME: 10 MINUTES
SERVES: 4

FOR THE CINNAMON SWIRL MIX

4 tablespoons (½ stick) vegan
   butter, melted
½ cup packed brown sugar
2 teaspoons ground cinnamon

FOR THE PANCAKE BATTER

1¼ cups all-purpose flour
1 teaspoon baking powder
¼ teaspoon baking soda
⅛ teaspoon salt
1 cup unsweetened nondairy milk
2 tablespoons water
Vegan butter and maple syrup,
   for topping

TOOLS/EQUIPMENT

- 2 mixing bowls: 1 medium, 1 large
- Measuring cups and spoons
- Fork or whisk
- Chef's squeeze bottle or
  measuring cup with spout
- Spoon
- Large skillet
- Ladle or large spoon
- Flat turning spatula

**Prepare the cinnamon swirl mix.**
In a medium mixing bowl, combine the melted butter, brown sugar, and cinnamon. Using a fork or a whisk, mix everything, and make sure there are no clumps. Pour the swirl mix into a chef's squeeze bottle.

**Mix the pancake batter.**
In a large mixing bowl, stir together the flour, baking powder, baking soda, and salt until completely combined. Slowly pour in the milk and water and mix just until smooth. Some very small lumps are okay. You don't want to overmix the batter.

**Cook the pancakes.**
Heat a heavy skillet over medium-high heat. You'll know the skillet is hot enough when you sprinkle in a few drops of water and they "dance" across the skillet. Using a ladle, transfer the batter about ¼ cup at a time to the skillet. Don't crowd the skillet; only make as many pancakes at once as will fit easily (usually 2 or 4, depending on the size of your skillet). While the first side of the pancakes cook, use the squeeze bottle to decorate the pancakes. When bubbles appear and begin to pop, after about 2 minutes, it's time to flip the pancakes. Flip and cook for 1 to 2 minutes, or until golden brown on the bottom. Remove from the heat.

**Serve.**

Serve the pancakes, swirl-side up, with butter, maple syrup, or leftover cinnamon swirl mix!

 HELPFUL HINT: Drawing the swirls neatly takes practice, so make whatever designs you like best. Hearts, stars, and even squiggles all taste delicious!

Fruity Sheet Pan Pancakes

# Fruity Sheet Pan Pancakes

Nonstick cooking spray,
    for coating
2 ripe bananas, peeled
2½ cups nondairy milk
½ cup unsweetened applesauce
1 teaspoon vanilla extract
2½ cups whole-wheat flour
1 teaspoon ground cinnamon
1 teaspoon baking powder
½ teaspoon baking soda
½ teaspoon salt
1 cup sliced fresh strawberries
1 cup fresh blueberries
Optional toppings: Vegan butter,
    maple syrup, extra strawberries,
    and extra blueberries

### TOOLS/EQUIPMENT

- Cutting board
- Knife
- Large rimmed baking sheet
- Parchment paper
- 2 large mixing bowls
- Fork
- Measuring cups and spoons
- Whisk
- Rubber/silicone spatula
- Oven mitts or pot holders
- Flat turning spatula

**Turn on the oven and prep your baking sheet.**
Preheat the oven to 425°F. Line a large rimmed baking sheet with parchment paper and lightly coat it with cooking spray.

**Mix the wet ingredients.**
In a large mixing bowl, mash the bananas using the back of a fork until smooth. Add the milk, applesauce, and vanilla. Whisk until combined (some small banana lumps are okay).

**Mix the dry ingredients and combine.**
In a separate large mixing bowl, combine the flour, cinnamon, baking powder, baking soda, and salt. Slowly add the dry ingredients to the wet ingredients, stirring as you go. (I like to use a rubber spatula for this, which helps you scrape the sides of the bowl.) You want everything mixed completely, but do not overmix the batter. When the batter is combined, gently stir in the strawberries and blueberries.

**Bake.**
Pour the batter onto the prepared baking sheet, using a rubber spatula to spread it evenly. Transfer it to the oven and bake for 10 to 12 minutes, or until the top is light golden brown and the pancake has cooked all the way through. Using oven mitts, remove it from the oven. »

**Cut and serve.**

Using a turning spatula, cut individual pancakes and transfer them to plates. Serve with your favorite toppings.

 TRY INSTEAD: Replace the strawberries and blueberries with your favorite fruits.

HELPFUL HINT: These pancakes make fantastic leftovers! Simply store them in an airtight container in the refrigerator for up to 3 days and reheat when you're ready to enjoy.

# Blueberry French Toast Casserole

**PREP TIME:** 20 MINUTES
**COOK TIME:** 1 HOUR
**SERVES:** 6

½ loaf day-old French bread
(2 days old is best)
1 banana, peeled
1 (13½-ounce) can light
coconut milk
3 tablespoons pure maple syrup
1 teaspoon vanilla extract
½ teaspoon salt
2 cups fresh blueberries

TOOLS/EQUIPMENT

- Cutting board
- Serrated knife (optional)
- Large mixing bowl
- Fork
- Can opener
- Measuring cups and spoons
- 2-quart baking dish
- Oven mitts or pot holders

**Turn on the oven and cut the bread.**
Place a rack in the center of the oven and pre-heat the oven to 350°F. Cut or tear the bread into 1-inch cubes (it doesn't need to be exact). You want 7 rounded cups, which is about half of a loaf.

**Mix the ingredients.**
In a large mixing bowl, mash the banana using the back of a fork. Mix in the coconut milk, maple syrup, vanilla, and salt. Add the bread and blueberries. Gently stir to mix. You don't want the bread cubes to break apart too much.

**Bake the casserole.**
Pour the mixture into the baking dish. Place it on the center rack and bake for 50 minutes to 1 hour, or until the top is very lightly browned and the inside has firmed up. Using oven mitts, remove the casserole from the oven.

TROUBLESHOOTING: Did your casserole turn out a little mushy? Try using bread that is more dried out next time, which holds together better while baking.

Breakfast Tacos

# Breakfast Tacos

PREP TIME: 15 MINUTES, PLUS TIME TO PRESS THE TOFU
COOK TIME: 15 MINUTES
SERVES: 2

1 bell pepper, any color
½ sweet onion
2 tablespoons water, plus more as needed
1 (14-ounce) block firm tofu, well pressed (see page 23)
½ teaspoon kala namak salt
¼ cup nondairy milk
½ teaspoon red pepper flakes
½ teaspoon ground cumin
⅛ teaspoon freshly ground black pepper
4 small tortillas
Salsa, for topping
Optional toppings: Shredded vegan cheese, hot sauce, sliced avocado

**TOOLS/EQUIPMENT**

- Clean kitchen towels or tofu press
- Cutting board(s)
- Knife
- Measuring cups and spoons
- Large skillet
- Rubber/silicone spatula
- Small mixing bowl

**Prep and cook the veggies.**

Dice the bell pepper and onion. In a large skillet, heat the water over medium-high heat until it bubbles. Add the bell pepper and onion. Cook for 4 to 5 minutes, or until the vegetables are mostly soft, adding an extra tablespoon of water if the skillet dries out. Reduce the heat to medium-low. Using a rubber spatula, push the veggies to the outer edge of the skillet (in a big circle with an empty space in the center).

**Make the taco filling.**

Using your clean hands, crumble the tofu into a small mixing bowl. When it's in small pieces, add it to the center of the skillet and sprinkle with the kala namak salt. Give it a stir, keeping it as separate from the veggies as you can (but it is okay if a bit gets mixed in). Add the milk, red pepper flakes, cumin, and black pepper to the tofu. Stir everything together, including the veggies. Cook, stirring occasionally using the rubber spatula, for about 5 minutes, letting the mixture get warm.

**Assemble the tacos.**

When the tofu mix is warm, lay the tortillas on plates. Remove the skillet from the heat. Add one-fourth of the tofu mix to each tortilla and top with salsa or other toppings as you like. »

**PRO TIP:** Toast 4 slices of bread and smear them with mashed avocado. Top with the tofu scramble, and it's the perfect brunch treat!

**DID YOU KNOW?** In the United States, October 4th is National Taco Day! Serve these Breakfast Tacos for breakfast or lunch to celebrate!

# Baked Tempeh Bacon

**PREP TIME:** 10 MINUTES, PLUS 10 MINUTES TO MARINATE
**COOK TIME:** 15 MINUTES
**SERVES:** 4

1 (8-ounce) package tempeh
⅓ cup soy sauce
¼ cup real maple syrup
1 tablespoon smoked paprika
2 teaspoons avocado oil or olive oil
½ teaspoon garlic powder
½ teaspoon freshly ground black pepper

**TOOLS/EQUIPMENT**

- Large rimmed baking sheet
- Parchment paper
- Cutting board
- Knife
- Medium mixing bowl
- Measuring cups and spoons
- Whisk
- Flat turning spatula
- Oven mitts or pot holders

**Turn on the oven and prep your baking sheet.**
Preheat the oven to 350°F. Line a large rimmed baking sheet with parchment paper.

**Slice the tempeh.**
Cut the tempeh into 2 equal rectangles, then cut each rectangle into 2 so you have 4 equal pieces. Cut each of those pieces into 4 slices so you have 16 thin slices.

**Mix the marinade.**
In a medium mixing bowl, whisk together the soy sauce, maple syrup, paprika, avocado oil, garlic powder, and pepper until well combined. Add the tempeh slices to the bowl and let them soak for 5 to 10 minutes.

**Cook the bacon.**
Place the tempeh slices in a single layer on the prepared baking sheet. Cover with about half of the marinade (save the rest for later). Put the tempeh into the oven and bake for 8 minutes. Flip the pieces and top with the remaining marinade. Bake for 7 minutes, or until slightly crispy. Using oven mitts, remove it from the oven.

TRY INSTEAD: Use gluten-free tempeh and gluten-free soy sauce, or tamari, to make this bacon entirely gluten-free!

# Egg-Like Tofu Breakfast Sandwiches

**PREP TIME:** 10 MINUTES, PLUS TIME TO PRESS THE TOFU
**COOK TIME:** 10 MINUTES
**SERVES:** 4

1 (14-ounce) block firm tofu, well pressed (see page 23)
1 teaspoon Italian seasoning
½ teaspoon kala namak salt
¼ teaspoon ground turmeric
1 teaspoon avocado oil or olive oil
4 whole-wheat English muffins
Vegan butter, for spreading
4 vegan cheese slices

## TOOLS/EQUIPMENT

- Cutting board(s)
- Knife
- Clean kitchen towels or tofu press
- Small mixing bowl
- Measuring cups and spoons
- Spoon
- Large skillet
- Flat turning spatula
- Toaster

**Prepare the tofu.**

Cut the tofu in half across the short side, then in half again through the middle of the 2 pieces, making 4 thin rectangles. Lay the rectangles in a single layer on a cutting board. In a small mixing bowl, stir together the Italian seasoning, kala namak salt, and turmeric. Using a spoon, sprinkle about half of the spice mixture onto the tofu pieces, then using the back of the spoon or your fingers, rub it in. Flip the tofu and do the same on the other side with the remaining spice mixture.

**Cook the tofu.**

Heat a large skillet over medium heat. Pour in the avocado oil and heat until it shimmers—that means it is ready! Carefully place the tofu in the hot skillet and cook for 3 to 4 minutes, or until the bottom is light golden brown. Flip and cook for 3 to 4 minutes, or until light golden. Remove from the heat.

**Assemble the sandwiches.**

While the tofu cooks, toast the English muffins, then spread butter on them. Pile on the eggy tofu and top each with a slice of cheese. Serve hot.

> **TRY INSTEAD:** There is no limit to the toppings you can add to this breakfast sandwich. Try adding Baked Tempeh Bacon (page 47) or some maple syrup, sliced avocado, or a schmear of vegan mayonnaise.

Yogurt, Granola, and Fruit Parfait

# Yogurt, Granola, and Fruit Parfait

**PREP TIME:** 25 MINUTES
**COOK TIME:** 20 MINUTES
**SERVES:** 4

## FOR THE GRANOLA

¼ cup coconut oil
¼ cup real maple syrup
¼ teaspoon vanilla extract
¼ teaspoon salt
¼ teaspoon ground cinnamon
1½ cups old-fashioned oats
½ cup pecans
½ cup raisins

## FOR THE PARFAIT

2 bananas
1 cup fresh blueberries
2 cups vegan vanilla
     yogurt, divided

## TOOLS/EQUIPMENT

- Large rimmed baking sheet
- Parchment paper
- Mixing bowls: 1 large, 1 small
- Measuring cups and spoons
- Rubber/silicone spatula
- Oven mitts or pot holders
- Wire rack
- Cutting board
- Knife
- 4 medium or large drinking glasses

**Turn on the oven and prep your baking sheet.**
Preheat the oven to 300°F. Line a large rimmed baking sheet with parchment paper.

**Make the granola mixture.**
In a large mixing bowl, combine the coconut oil, maple syrup, vanilla, salt, and cinnamon. Using a rubber spatula, stir to mix well. Add the oats and pecans. Continue to stir until the ingredients are completely coated.

**Bake the granola.**
Spread the granola out in an even layer on the prepared baking sheet. Using the back of a large spoon or a spatula, press it into the sheet. Transfer the granola to the oven and bake for 10 minutes. Stir the granola gently, then bake for 10 more minutes, or until the granola is light golden brown. It will still be a little soft, but will crisp as it cools. Using oven mitts, remove the granola from the oven.

**Add the fruit and cool.**
Move the baking sheet to a wire rack to cool. Sprinkle the raisins across the top of the granola, and using the back of a large spoon or a spatula, press down one more time. Let cool completely before storing or adding to the parfaits. »

**Peel and slice the bananas.**

Remove the banana peels completely. Halve the bananas lengthwise, then cut into thin half-moons. Transfer to a small mixing bowl. Add the blueberries.

**Layer the parfaits.**

Set out 4 drinking glasses for serving. Scoop ¼ cup of yogurt into each glass. Evenly divide about half of the granola among the glasses, spooning it over the yogurt. Evenly divide about half of the fruit among the glasses, spooning it over the granola. Repeat with the remaining yogurt, granola, and fruit, then serve.

DID YOU KNOW? Granola may taste like dessert, but it's actually good for you. It has a lot of fiber from the oats and can help keep you full all morning!

Breaded No-Chicken Nuggets (page 56)

# 4

# Snacks & Bites

# Breaded No-Chicken Nuggets

**PREP TIME:** 15 MINUTES, PLUS TIME TO PRESS THE TOFU
**COOK TIME:** 30 MINUTES
**SERVES:** 6

1 (14-ounce) block extra-firm tofu, well pressed (see page 23)
½ cup unsweetened nondairy milk
1 tablespoon cornstarch
¾ cup panko bread crumbs
2 tablespoons Montreal Chicken Seasoning
1 teaspoon paprika
½ teaspoon salt
Optional: Sauce for dipping, such as ketchup, barbecue sauce, or vegan ranch dressing

## TOOLS/EQUIPMENT

- Clean kitchen towels or tofu press
- Large rimmed baking sheet
- Parchment paper
- Cutting board(s)
- Knife
- 2 shallow bowls
- Measuring cups and spoons
- Whisk
- Spoon
- Tongs
- Oven mitts or pot holders

**Turn on the oven and prep your baking sheet.**
Preheat the oven to 400°F. Line a large rimmed baking sheet with parchment paper.

**Prepare the tofu and breading station.**
Cut the tofu into about 30 cubes, all the same size. Set out 2 shallow bowls. In one bowl, whisk together the milk and cornstarch until the cornstarch dissolves; in the other bowl, stir together the bread crumbs, Montreal seasoning, paprika, and salt. Place the tofu on a cutting board in front of you. Place the milk-cornstarch mixture and bread crumb mixture to the right of the cutting board. Place the prepared baking sheet to the right of the bowls.

**Coat the nuggets.**
Using just one hand, dip a tofu cube one at a time in the milk mixture. Make sure all sides are wet, then drop it into the bread crumb mixture. Switch hands and turn the tofu cube until it's covered on all sides by bread crumbs, pressing the cube firmly into them to help them stick. (Using a different hand for each coating helps keep you and your workspace neat.) Put each coated cube on the baking sheet. »

**Bake.**

Transfer the baking sheet to the oven and bake for 15 minutes. Using tongs, turn the cubes over. Bake for 15 more minutes, or until the cubes are lightly browned. Using oven mitts, remove the nuggets from the oven. Let sit for 5 minutes before serving with your favorite dipping sauce.

PRO TIP: Montreal Chicken Seasoning is a blend of several spices. Make your own: In a small mixing bowl, stir together 1½ teaspoons dried parsley flakes, 1 teaspoon garlic powder, 1 teaspoon onion powder, 1 teaspoon ground coriander, ½ teaspoon paprika, ½ teaspoon ground turmeric, ¼ teaspoon salt, ¼ teaspoon freshly ground black pepper, and a pinch chili powder, any kind. Store in a sealed container.

Spinach and Red Pepper Hummus Melts

# Spinach and Red Pepper Hummus Melts

**PREP TIME:** 20 MINUTES

**COOK TIME:** 10 MINUTES

**SERVES:** 2

2 whole-grain English muffins

½ bell pepper, any color

2 tablespoons water, plus more as needed

1 cup fresh baby spinach

½ cup hummus

¼ cup shredded vegan mozzarella cheese (optional)

**TOOLS/EQUIPMENT**

- Toaster
- Cutting board
- Knife
- Skillet
- Baking sheet
- Measuring cups and spoons
- Oven mitts or pot holders

**Prep the ingredients.**

Split the English muffins and lightly toast them. Meanwhile, chop the bell pepper into small bite-size pieces.

**Sauté the vegetables.**

In a skillet, heat the water over medium-high heat. Add the bell pepper and spinach. Cook, stirring occasionally, for 5 to 6 minutes, or until the spinach wilts and the bell pepper is slightly soft. Add another tablespoon of water if the skillet gets dry. Remove from the heat.

**Assemble the melts.**

Put the English muffins on a baking sheet and slather evenly with the hummus. Top each with the vegetables and cheese (if using).

**Broil.**

Preheat the broiler on low heat. Place the baking sheet on the middle rack in the oven and broil for 1 to 2 minutes, checking every 30 seconds. You want the veggies to toast, not burn. Once the tops are nicely browned, using oven mitts, carefully remove the baking sheet from the oven. Let the melts cool for a few minutes before serving.

MIX IT UP: Put your favorite veggies on top of these melts—sliced carrot and chopped kale are two I like to add—and add some vegan mozzarella if you like!

Chipotle–Sweet Potato Dip

# Chipotle–Sweet Potato Dip

**PREP TIME:** 10 MINUTES, PLUS 1 HOUR TO SOAK THE CASHEWS
**COOK TIME:** 10 MINUTES
**SERVES:** 6

½ cup raw cashew pieces
Boiling water, to soak the cashews
1 sweet potato
¼ cup water
½ cup unsweetened nondairy milk
¼ teaspoon salt
⅛ teaspoon chipotle powder
⅛ teaspoon smoked paprika
Optional: Raw veggies or crackers, for serving

TOOLS/EQUIPMENT

- Measuring cups and spoons
- Medium mixing bowl
- Colander
- Peeler
- Cutting board
- Knife
- Microwave-safe bowl
- Food processor or blender
- Spoon

**Soak the cashews.**
Put the cashews in a medium mixing bowl and pour in enough boiling water to cover them. Cover the bowl and let it sit for 1 hour. Place a colander in the sink and drain and rinse the cashews in it.

**Cook the sweet potato.**
While the cashews soak, peel the sweet potato and cut it into 1-inch pieces. (Cutting raw sweet potato can be difficult, so ask an adult for help.) Transfer it to a microwave-safe bowl. Add the water. Cover the bowl and microwave on high power for 5 minutes. Stir, re-cover the bowl, and microwave for 2 to 3 minutes, or until the sweet potato is soft. Drain the sweet potato and set aside to cool.

**Blend the cashews.**
Put the drained cashew pieces and milk in a food processor or blender. Process for 2 to 3 minutes, or until smooth. Using a spoon, scoop half of the cashew mix (it doesn't need to be exact) into a bowl.

**Blend the dip.**
Add the sweet potato to the remaining cashew mix in the food processor, along with the salt, chipotle powder, and paprika. Process for 1 to 2 minutes, or until smooth, adding the scooped-out cashew mix as you go until you reach your desired consistency. »

**Serve.**

Scoop the dip into a bowl and serve with raw veggies or crackers.

 HELPFUL HINT: Not all food processors are the same. When blending small amounts of an ingredient, such as cashew pieces, you need a food processor with blades positioned at or near the bottom of the bowl. If you have a mini food processor, it would work well for this recipe.

# Creamy Buffalo Cauliflower Dip

**PREP TIME:** 10 MINUTES
**COOK TIME:** 15 MINUTES
**SERVES:** 4

2 rounded cups small
    cauliflower florets
⅓ cup Buffalo sauce
1 (15-ounce) can chickpeas
¼ cup nondairy milk, plus more
    as needed
¼ teaspoon salt
¼ teaspoon garlic powder
¼ teaspoon onion powder
Optional: Raw carrots, celery,
    and/or crackers, for serving

**TOOLS/EQUIPMENT**

- Large rimmed baking sheet
- Parchment paper
- 2 large mixing bowls
- Measuring cups and spoons
- Oven mitts or pot holders
- Colander
- Can opener
- Spoon
- Food processor

**Turn on the oven and prep your baking sheet.**
Preheat the oven to 400°F. Line a large rimmed baking sheet with parchment paper.

**Season and roast the cauliflower.**
In a large mixing bowl, stir together the cauliflower and Buffalo sauce to coat. Spread the cauliflower out on the prepared baking sheet. Transfer it to the oven and bake for 10 minutes. Stir, then bake for 5 more minutes, or until tender. Using oven mitts, remove the cauliflower from the oven.

**Prepare the dip.**
Place a colander over another large mixing bowl. Pour the chickpeas into the colander, letting the liquid (called "aquafaba") drain into the bowl. Set the aquafaba aside, then rinse and drain the chickpeas. Put the chickpeas, 3 tablespoons of the aquafaba, the milk, salt, garlic powder, and onion powder in a food processor. (If you don't have a food processor, use a blender.) Process for about 1 minute, or until completely smooth. Add another tablespoon of milk if the dip is too thick. Transfer to a mixing bowl (use the one you combined the cauliflower and Buffalo sauce in) and fold in the cauliflower. Serve with raw carrots, celery, and/or crackers.

> DID YOU KNOW? The word "aquafaba" is from the Latin "aqua" (water) and "faba" (bean). It can be used as an egg substitute when baking.

# Loaded Almond Butter Toast

PREP TIME: 5 MINUTES
COOK TIME: 5 MINUTES
SERVES: 2

2 bread slices

¼ cup walnut halves

2 to 4 tablespoons almond butter (depending on how large your bread slices are)

24 to 26 fresh blueberries

2 teaspoons sweetened coconut flakes

⅛ teaspoon ground cinnamon, plus more as needed

### TOOLS/EQUIPMENT

- Toaster
- Measuring cups and spoons
- Cutting board
- Knife

**Prepare the ingredients.**

Toast the bread. Finely chop the walnuts.

**Layer the toast.**

Lay the pieces of toast out on your plates. Gently cover each slice with almond butter, then sprinkle with the chopped walnuts. Add the blueberries, and using your fingers, gently push them into the almond butter. Top with the coconut flakes and cinnamon.

> PRO TIP: If you're using an all-natural almond butter that doesn't have a lot of salt in it, add a pinch to each slice of toast before adding the toppings.

# Almond Butter No-Bake Snack Balls

**PREP TIME:** 15 MINUTES, PLUS 45 MINUTES TO CHILL

**SERVES:** 6

1⅓ cups old-fashioned oats (make sure they are labeled gluten-free if you avoid gluten)

½ cup almond butter, such as Justin's classic

¼ cup real maple syrup

2 tablespoons unsweetened coconut flakes

1 teaspoon vanilla extract

⅛ teaspoon salt

¼ teaspoon ground cinnamon

### TOOLS/EQUIPMENT

- Measuring cups and spoons
- Medium mixing bowl
- Mixing spoon or rubber/silicone spatula
- Plastic wrap
- Large rimmed baking sheet

**Mix the ingredients and chill.**

In a medium mixing bowl, stir together the oats, almond butter, maple syrup, coconut flakes, vanilla, salt, and cinnamon. Cover the bowl with plastic wrap and refrigerate for 30 minutes.

**Form the snack balls.**

Using your clean hands, roll the chilled mixture into about 1-inch balls. Squeeze them tightly so they won't fall apart.

**Chill the snack balls.**

Put the balls on a large rimmed baking sheet and refrigerate for 15 minutes.

**Serve.**

Enjoy the snack balls right from the refrigerator. Extras can be refrigerated in an airtight container for up to 4 days or frozen for up to 2 months.

> TRY INSTEAD: If you don't like almond butter, use peanut butter or sunflower seed butter instead.

# Apple-Oat Bars

**PREP TIME:** 15 MINUTES
**COOK TIME:** 25 MINUTES
**SERVES:** 10

Nonstick cooking spray, for coating the baking dish

1 tablespoon chia seeds

2½ tablespoons water

2 or 3 medium apples, such as Gala or Fuji

3 cups old-fashioned oats (make sure they are labeled gluten-free if you avoid gluten)

2 teaspoons ground cinnamon

2 teaspoons baking powder

½ teaspoon salt

¼ teaspoon ground nutmeg

1 cup unsweetened nondairy milk

⅓ cup real maple syrup

½ cup unsweetened applesauce

1½ teaspoons vanilla extract

## TOOLS/EQUIPMENT

- 9-by-13-inch baking dish
- Measuring cups and spoons
- Mixing bowls: 2 small, 1 large
- Peeler
- Spoon
- Cutting board
- Knife
- Whisk
- Rubber/silicone spatula
- Oven mitts or pot holders

**Turn on the oven and prep your baking dish.**
Put a rack in the middle position in the oven and preheat the oven to 375°F. Lightly coat a 9-by-13-inch baking dish with cooking spray.

**Mix your chia "egg."**
In a small mixing bowl, stir together the chia seeds and water to combine. This creates an egg substitute called a "chia egg."

**Chop the apples.**
Peel and core the apples, then cut them into smallish bite-size pieces to get about 2 rounded cups.

**Mix the ingredients.**
In a large mixing bowl, combine the apples, oats, cinnamon, baking powder, salt, and nutmeg. In another small mixing bowl, whisk together the milk, maple syrup, applesauce, vanilla, and chia egg to blend. Slowly add the wet ingredients to the dry ingredients, using a rubber spatula to scrape the sticky ingredients off the sides of the bowl. Transfer the mixture to the prepared baking dish, and using the flat edge of the spatula, pack it in as firmly as you can.

**Bake and serve.**
Place the baking dish on the middle rack in the oven and bake for 20 to 25 minutes, or until the top is light golden brown. Using oven mitts, remove the bars from the oven. Let cool for 5 to 10 minutes before serving.

# Strawberry, Banana, and Peanut Butter Quesadillas

**PREP TIME:** 10 MINUTES
**COOK TIME:** 5 MINUTES
**SERVES:** 1

1 small banana or ½ medium
   banana
2 fresh strawberries
2 tablespoons peanut butter
1 (10-inch) flour tortilla

TOOLS/EQUIPMENT

- Cutting board
- Knife
- Measuring spoons
- Large nonstick skillet
- Flat turning spatula

**Slice the fruit.**
Peel the banana and cut into thin circles. Remove any green from the tops of the strawberries, then thinly slice the strawberries.

**Build the quesadilla.**
Spread the peanut butter evenly onto one side of the tortilla. Place the tortilla in a large non-stick skillet, peanut butter–side up, then sprinkle the fruit evenly across half of it. Carefully fold the side of the tortilla without fruit over the fruit-filled side.

**Cook and serve the quesadilla.**
Place the skillet on the stovetop over medium heat. Cook for 2 minutes, or until the bottom is light golden brown and the peanut butter has started to get gooey. Using a turning spatula, carefully flip the tortilla and cook the other side for 60 to 90 seconds. Remove it from the skillet. Let it cool for 1 to 2 minutes before eating.

> MIX IT UP: Use a flavored brand of peanut or almond butter, like chocolate or vanilla, to change up the flavor a little bit.

Avocado and Tomato Grilled Cheese Sandwiches (page 80)

# 5

# Soups, Salads & Sandwiches

# Taco Soup

PREP TIME: 10 MINUTES
COOK TIME: 25 TO 30 MINUTES
SERVES: 4

1 green bell pepper
½ sweet onion
3 tablespoons water, plus
    2½ to 3 cups, divided
1 (15-ounce) can black beans
1 (15-ounce) can mild chili beans
1 (15-ounce) can diced tomatoes
1 cup frozen sweet corn
1 teaspoon ground cumin
½ teaspoon garlic powder
½ teaspoon salt
½ teaspoon smoked paprika
¼ teaspoon chili powder
1 cup tortilla chips, slightly crushed
    (use gluten-free if you are
    avoiding gluten)
Optional toppings: Sliced jalapeño
    pepper, sliced scallion, vegan
    sour cream, vegan shredded
    cheese of choice

### TOOLS/EQUIPMENT

- Cutting board
- Knife
- Large pot with lid
- Can opener
- Colander
- Wooden spoon or
  rubber/silicone spatula
- Measuring cups and spoons

**Dice and sauté the veggies.**

Dice the bell pepper and onion. Heat a large pot over medium-high heat. Add 3 tablespoons water, the bell pepper, and onion. Cook, stirring constantly using a wooden spoon, for 2 to 3 minutes, adding an extra tablespoon of water if the pot dries out.

**Make the soup.**

Drain and rinse the black beans. Do not drain or rinse the chili beans. To the pot, add the black beans, chili beans, tomatoes with their juices, corn, cumin, garlic powder, salt, paprika, chili powder, and 2 cups water. Bring to a boil, then reduce the heat to medium. Cover the pot and simmer, stirring occasionally (be careful of the hot steam when you remove the lid), for 20 minutes. If the soup gets too thick, add ½ cup to 1 cup more water. Remove from the heat.

**Top and serve.**

Spoon the soup into bowls. Top with the crushed tortilla chips and any other toppings you like.

PRO TIP: If you add jalapeños to the soup, remove the seeds first—that's where most of the heat is!

# Hearty Tomato Soup

**PREP TIME:** 5 MINUTES
**COOK TIME:** 25 MINUTES
**SERVES:** 4

6 ounces orzo
1 (28-ounce) can diced tomatoes
¾ cup unsweetened nondairy milk
2 tablespoons vegan butter
1 teaspoon sugar
½ teaspoon salt, plus more
    for seasoning
½ teaspoon onion powder
¼ teaspoon garlic powder
⅛ teaspoon freshly ground
    black pepper

TOOLS/EQUIPMENT

- Medium stockpot
- Colander
- Can opener
- Blender
- Measuring cups and spoons
- Wooden spoon or
  rubber/silicone spatula

**Cook the pasta.**
In a medium stockpot, cook the orzo according to the package instructions, minus 2 minutes. Remove from the heat. Place a colander in the sink and drain the orzo in it. Return it to the pot.

**Blend the tomatoes.**
Drain the tomatoes in the colander and pour them into the blender. Blend on high speed for 10 to 12 seconds. The mixture should be smooth, but some tiny pieces are okay.

**Combine the pasta and sauce.**
Pour the blended tomatoes into the pot with the pasta. Stir in the milk, butter, sugar, salt, onion powder, garlic powder, and pepper.

**Cook.**
Place the pot on the stovetop and bring to a boil over high heat. Reduce the heat to low. Simmer, stirring often, for 15 minutes. Taste, adding more salt if you think it needs it. Remove the pot from the heat.

HELPFUL HINT: When cooking anything tomato based, it's a good idea to wear an apron and use a slightly larger pan or pot than needed to protect yourself (and the kitchen!) from splatter stains.

# Great Big Tofu Salad

PREP TIME: 15 MINUTES, PLUS 20 MINUTES TO MARINATE THE TOFU
COOK TIME: 35 MINUTES
SERVES: 4

**FOR THE TOFU**

Nonstick cooking spray, for coating

1 tablespoon soy sauce

1 tablespoon rice vinegar

1 tablespoon real maple syrup

1 tablespoon water

1 tablespoon sesame oil

1 (14-ounce) block firm tofu, well pressed (see page 23)

**FOR THE SALAD**

1 large head romaine lettuce

1 red bell pepper

1 scallion, green and white parts

1 carrot

½ cucumber

1 cup grape tomatoes

1 ripe avocado

Juice of ½ lime

½ cup favorite salad dressing, plus more as needed

Optional salad toppings: Sliced mushrooms, sliced radishes, vegan shredded cheese of choice

**Turn on the oven and prep your baking sheet.**
Preheat the oven to 420°F. Lightly coat a large rimmed baking sheet with cooking spray.

**Marinate the tofu.**
In a medium mixing bowl, whisk together the soy sauce, vinegar, maple syrup, water, and sesame oil to blend. Cut the tofu into bite-size cubes and add to the bowl. Let it marinate for about 20 minutes, then put the tofu in a single layer on the prepared baking sheet.

**Bake the tofu.**
Transfer the baking sheet to the oven and bake for 20 minutes. Using oven mitts, carefully remove the baking sheet from the oven and spritz the top of the tofu cubes with cooking spray. Using tongs, flip the tofu. Using oven mitts again, return the baking sheet to the oven and bake for 10 to 15 minutes, or until the tofu is light golden brown and slightly puffy. Using oven mitts again, move the baking sheet to a wire rack. Let it cool a little before adding the tofu to the salad.

**Prepare the salad greens.**
Chop the romaine lettuce into bite-size pieces. Put them in a large mixing bowl.

**Cut the vegetables.**
Dice the red bell pepper and thinly slice the scallion. Peel the carrot and cut it into circles. Add the bell pepper, scallion, and carrot to the salad bowl. Halve the cucumber lengthwise, then cut it into thin half-moons. Add the cucumber and tomatoes to the salad bowl.

- Clean kitchen towels or tofu press
- Cutting board(s)
- Large rimmed baking sheet
- Mixing bowls: 1 medium, 1 large
- Whisk
- Measuring cups and spoons
- Knife
- Oven mitts or pot holders
- Tongs
- Wire rack
- Peeler
- Spoon

**Halve the avocado.**

Cut the avocado lengthwise around the seed (ask an adult for help). Gently hold on to each side and twist until they separate. Be careful not to squeeze too hard, or you'll bruise the fruit. Slide the tip of a spoon underneath the seed, then scoop out the seed and throw it away. Turn the avocado halves facedown on your cutting board and peel away the skin. Cut both halves lengthwise into thin slices, then across the slices to dice. Pour the lime juice over the avocado. (You can throw the juiced lime half away.)

**Toss the salad.**

Add the tofu and dressing to the salad bowl. Using tongs, gently toss the salad until everything is evenly mixed (adding more dressing if necessary). The thicker your dressing, the more you may need. Top with the diced avocado and toss one last time to serve.

FUN FACT: In some parts of the world, avocados are called "alligator pears" or "butter fruit."

Southwestern Sweet Potato Salad

# Southwestern Sweet Potato Salad

**PREP TIME:** 25 MINUTES, PLUS TIME TO CHILL THE SWEET POTATOES

**COOK TIME:** 10 MINUTES

**SERVES:** 6

3 sweet potatoes

½ cup vegan mayonnaise

½ teaspoon ground cumin

½ teaspoon salt

1 teaspoon freshly squeezed lime juice

1 (15-ounce) can black beans

1 red bell pepper

1 celery stalk

**TOOLS/EQUIPMENT**

- Peeler
- Cutting board
- Knife
- Medium pot
- Fork
- Colander
- Measuring cups and spoons
- Mixing bowls: 1 medium, 1 small, 1 large
- Spoon

**Prepare the sweet potatoes.**

Peel the sweet potatoes and chop them into bite-size pieces. You want all the pieces to be about the same size so they cook evenly.

**Boil the sweet potatoes.**

Put the sweet potatoes in a medium pot and cover them with water. Bring to a boil over high heat. Cook, stirring occasionally, for 6 to 8 minutes, or until the sweet potatoes pierce easily with a fork. Remove from the heat. Place a colander in the sink and drain the sweet potatoes in it. Rinse with cold water. Transfer them to a medium mixing bowl. Cover the bowl and refrigerate until chilled.

**Mix the dressing.**

In a small mixing bowl, stir together the mayonnaise, cumin, salt, and lime juice. »

**Prepare the rest of the ingredients and assemble the salad.**

Drain and rinse the black beans, then pour them into a large mixing bowl. Dice the red bell pepper and celery and add to the beans. When the sweet potatoes have cooled completely, add to the bowl, then stir in the dressing. (It may seem like a lot of dressing at first, but some will soak into the sweet potatoes.) Refrigerate until ready to serve. Stir one more time before you spoon the salad onto plates.

FUN FACT: In some parts of the United States, sweet potatoes are called yams, but they are actually very different from yams. Sweet potatoes have thin, smooth skin and are flavorful and moist, whereas yams have rough, dark skin and are often starchy and dry.

# Veggie Pasta Salad

**PREP TIME:** 15 MINUTES
**COOK TIME:** 15 MINUTES
**SERVES:** 4

3 cups pasta shells

1 cup frozen peas, thawed

1 red bell pepper

2 carrots

¼ cup olive oil

3 tablespoons red-wine vinegar

½ teaspoon salt, plus more
    for seasoning

⅛ teaspoon freshly ground
    black pepper, plus more
    for seasoning

⅛ teaspoon garlic powder

## TOOLS/EQUIPMENT

- Medium saucepan with lid
- Colander
- Measuring cups and spoons
- Mixing bowls: 1 large, 1 small
- Cutting board
- Knife
- Box grater or food processor

**Cook the pasta.**

In a medium saucepan, cook the pasta shells according to the package instructions. Remove from the heat. Place a colander in the sink and drain the pasta shells in it. Rinse well with cold water. Shake off excess moisture.

**Prepare the veggies.**

Put the peas in a large mixing bowl. Dice the bell pepper and add it to the bowl. Using a box grater, shred the carrots and add them to the bowl.

**Make the dressing and combine.**

In a small bowl, stir together the olive oil, red-wine vinegar, salt, pepper, and garlic powder. Add the pasta shells to the large mixing bowl, then top with the dressing. Stir well to combine. Taste, adding more salt and pepper as needed.

> TRY INSTEAD: Lots of raw veggies would be good in this salad; just make sure they are cut or shredded into small pieces. I like sweet corn, broccoli florets, and grape tomatoes sliced in half best!

# Smashed Chickpea and Avocado Salad Sandwiches

**PREP TIME:** 15 MINUTES

**SERVES:** 4

1 ripe medium avocado

1 teaspoon freshly squeezed lime juice (about ½ lime)

½ teaspoon salt, plus more for seasoning

¼ teaspoon garlic powder

⅛ teaspoon freshly ground black pepper, plus more for seasoning

1 (15-ounce) can chickpeas

½ red bell pepper

2 tablespoons sweet relish

½ teaspoon Old Bay seasoning

8 whole-grain bread slices

Optional toppings: Mustard, sliced tomato, lettuce, potato chips

---

**TOOLS/EQUIPMENT**

- Cutting board
- Knife
- Spoon
- Mixing bowls: 1 small, 1 large
- Fork
- Measuring cups and spoons
- Can opener
- Colander
- Toaster

### Season the avocado.

Cut the avocado lengthwise around the seed (ask an adult for help). Gently hold on to each side and twist until they separate. Be careful not to squeeze too hard, or you'll bruise the fruit. Slide the tip of a spoon underneath the seed, then scoop out the seed and throw it away. Scrape the inside of the avocado into a small mixing bowl and mash using the back of a fork. Stir in the lime juice, salt, garlic powder, and pepper.

### Prep the chickpeas.

Drain and rinse the chickpeas. Pour them into a large mixing bowl and mash and break them apart using the back of a fork (this can be done more easily in a food processor, pulsing the chickpeas for 5 to 6 seconds). You want mostly small pieces, although a few larger chunks are okay.

### Dice the bell pepper.

Finely dice the red bell pepper and add it to the bowl with the chickpeas.

### Mix the salad.

Add the avocado mixture, relish, and Old Bay seasoning to the chickpeas. Stir until combined. Taste and see if you think it needs more salt or pepper.

**Make the sandwiches.**

Toast the bread. Scoop some of the salad onto 4 of the toast slices. Add your desired toppings and condiments and place another piece of toast on top of each sandwich. Cut the sandwiches in half and serve.

TROUBLESHOOTING: If you have leftover chickpea salad, put it in an airtight container and cover it with a piece of plastic wrap. Press the wrap down gently across the top of the salad so none of it is exposed to air, then add the container's cover. This will keep the avocado from turning brown.

# Avocado and Tomato Grilled Cheese Sandwiches

**PREP TIME:** 10 MINUTES
**COOK TIME:** 10 MINUTES
**SERVES:** 2

1 small tomato
1 ripe small avocado
6 teaspoons vegan butter (the
    kind in a tub works best),
    at room temperature
4 whole-grain bread slices
4 vegan cheddar or vegan white
    cheese slices

TOOLS/EQUIPMENT

- Cutting board
- Knife
- Spoon
- Large skillet
- Measuring cups and spoons
- Flat turning spatula

**Prep the veggies.**

Cut the tomato into thin circles. Cut the avocado lengthwise around the seed (ask an adult for help). Gently hold on to each side and twist until they separate. Be careful not to squeeze too hard, or you'll bruise the fruit. Slide the tip of a spoon underneath the seed, then scoop out the seed and throw it away. Turn the avocado halves facedown on your cutting board and peel away the skin. Cut both halves into thin slices.

**Assemble and cook the sandwiches.**

Heat a large skillet over medium-low heat. Spread 1½ teaspoons of butter on one side of each bread slice and place 2 slices, butter-side down, in the skillet. Layer on 1 cheese slice, 1 tomato slice, and about half of the avocado slices (you may not use all the avocado, depending on how big your bread is). Add another slice of cheese to each sandwich, then top each with a second slice of bread, butter-side up. Reduce the heat to low. Cook for 4 to 5 minutes, or until the bottom bread slices are golden brown. (Using the edge of a turning spatula, lift up a corner of each sandwich to check the bottom, being careful not to knock out the fillings.)

**Flip the sandwiches.**

When it is time to flip the sandwiches, slide the spatula under one of the sandwiches, place your fingertips on top of the sandwich to hold everything in place and gently turn the sandwich over so the browned side is up. Repeat with the second sandwich. Cook for 4 to 5 more minutes, or until these bottom bread slices are golden brown and the cheese has all melted. Remove from the heat.

HELPFUL HINT: The easiest way to tell if an avocado is ripe is to squeeze it gently. A ripe one will feel barely soft, not mushy.

# Sweet 'n' Spicy Tempeh Pita Pockets

**PREP TIME:** 20 MINUTES
**COOK TIME:** 1 MINUTE
**SERVES:** 4

1 (8-ounce) package tempeh
⅓ cup Thai sweet chili sauce, plus 2 tablespoons, divided
¼ cup vegan mayonnaise
2 carrots
12 dill pickle chips
4 individual pitas, or 2 large round pitas, halved
4 lettuce leaves

TOOLS/EQUIPMENT
- Microwave-safe bowl with lid
- Measuring cups and spoons
- Spoon
- Small mixing bowl
- Cutting board
- Knife
- Box grater or food processor

**Prepare the tempeh.**

Using your clean hands, crumble the tempeh into bite-size pieces and put them in a microwave-safe bowl. Stir in ⅓ cup Thai sweet chili sauce. Put the lid on the bowl and microwave on high power for 30 to 60 seconds, or until hot.

**Prepare the filling.**

In a small mixing bowl, stir together the mayonnaise and remaining 2 tablespoons of Thai sweet chili sauce. Grate the carrots—either by hand, using a box grater, or in a food processor (ask an adult for help). Halve the pickle chips.

**Assemble the wraps.**

Schmear about one-fourth of the mayonnaise mixture onto each pita. Add the lettuce, tempeh, and pickles. Top with the carrot. Stir the fillings together a little if you'd like, so there's a little bit of each flavor in every bite! Fold the pitas and serve.

**MIX IT UP:** Want to make it a little hotter? Add your favorite Asian hot sauce (like sriracha) to the tempeh and sweet chili sauce, ¼ teaspoon at a time. Be careful not to add too much, because you can't take it out!

**HELPFUL HINT:** You don't need to peel the carrots. In fact, many of a carrot's nutrients are found in the skin and immediately below it. Washing and drying them before eating is perfectly fine.

Spaghetti and Beanballs (page 107)

# 6

# Dinners & Family Feasts

# Teriyaki Roasted Tofu and Veggies

1 (14-ounce) container firm tofu,
    drained and pressed for
    30 minutes
6 tablespoons teriyaki
    sauce, divided
1 large sweet potato (about
    1 pound)
5 cups broccoli florets
3 tablespoons olive oil
¼ teaspoon salt
⅛ teaspoon freshly ground pepper

### TOOLS/EQUIPMENT

- Clean kitchen towels or tofu press
- Cutting board(s)
- Knife
- Large mixing bowl
- 11-by-17-inch baking sheet
- Oven mitts or pot holders
- Spatula or large spoon

**Marinate the tofu.**

Preheat the oven to 400°F. Cut the tofu into ¾-inch cubes and put them in a large mixing bowl. Top with 2 tablespoons teriyaki sauce and stir.

**Toss in oil and seasonings.**

Cut the sweet potato into ¾-inch dice. Add the sweet potato, broccoli, olive oil, salt, and pepper to the mixing bowl. Toss until evenly coated.

**Bake.**

Spread the veggie mixture in a single layer on an 11-by-17-inch baking sheet. Place on the middle rack in the oven and bake for 20 minutes. Using oven mitts, carefully pull the rack out of the oven so you can stir the tofu and veggies (ask for help if you need it!), then bake for 15 more minutes.

**Add the sauce.**

Using oven mitts, pull the rack out again. Top the tofu and veggies with the remaining 4 tablespoons of teriyaki sauce, then bake for 5 minutes. Using oven mitts again, remove the tofu mixture from the oven. Let cool for 4 to 5 minutes before serving.

PRO TIP: Before serving, top each serving with 1 tablespoon freshly sliced scallions or whatever fresh herbs you have on hand.

# Veggie Fajitas

PREP TIME: 25 MINUTES
COOK TIME: 5 MINUTES
SERVES: 4

**FOR THE SEASONING**

¼ teaspoon chili powder

¼ teaspoon ground cumin

¼ teaspoon onion powder

¼ teaspoon garlic powder

¼ teaspoon paprika

¼ teaspoon salt

⅛ teaspoon freshly ground
   black pepper

**FOR THE FAJITAS**

2 bell peppers, any color

1 sweet onion or red onion

1 small summer squash or zucchini

1 lime, halved

¼ cup water, plus more as needed

1 ripe avocado

8 (6-inch) tortillas

Optional toppings: Salsa, chopped
   fresh cilantro, vegan sour cream

**TOOLS/EQUIPMENT**

- Large mixing bowl
- Measuring cups and spoons
- Spoon
- Cutting board
- Knife
- Large skillet with lid

**Mix the fajita seasoning.**

In a large mixing bowl, stir together the chili powder, cumin, onion powder, garlic powder, paprika, salt, and pepper.

**Prepare the fajita veggies.**

Cut the bell peppers and onion into thin strips about 2 inches long. Slice the squash similarly. Add the bell peppers, onion, squash, and juice of 1 of the lime halves to the bowl. Stir to combine. Let sit for 5 to 10 minutes.

**Cook the veggies.**

In a large skillet, heat the water over medium heat. Add the seasoned veggies and any juice in the bowl. Cover the skillet and sauté, stirring occasionally, for 4 to 5 minutes, or until the veggies are tender. Add another tablespoon of water if the skillet dries out. Remove from the heat.

**Slice the avocado.**

Cut the avocado lengthwise around the seed (ask an adult for help). Gently hold on to each side and twist until they separate. Be careful not to squeeze too hard, or you'll bruise the fruit. Slide the tip of a spoon underneath the seed, then scoop out the seed and throw it away. Turn the avocado halves facedown on your cutting board and peel away the skin. Cut both halves into thin slices. Sprinkle with the juice of the remaining lime half. »

**Assemble the fajitas.**

Scoop the cooked veggies into the tortillas and top with the avocado and any other toppings you like.

MIX IT UP: There are no limits when it comes to what you can put in your fajitas. Sometimes I add diced sweet potatoes, broccoli florets, and even black beans.

# Rice and Bean Burritos

1 (15-ounce) can black beans
1 (15-ounce) can pinto beans
1 teaspoon ground cumin
½ teaspoon garlic powder
½ teaspoon chili powder (optional)
½ teaspoon salt
1 tablespoon water
2 cups cooked brown rice (either prepared in advance or microwavable, like Uncle Ben's)
¾ cup your favorite salsa
2 ripe avocados
6 large flour tortillas
Optional toppings: Chopped lettuce, additional salsa, hot sauce, vegan sour cream

## TOOLS/EQUIPMENT

- Medium skillet with lid
- Can opener
- Colander
- Measuring cups and spoons
- Cutting board
- Knife
- Spoon

**Prepare the filling.**

Heat a medium skillet over medium-low heat. Drain and rinse the black beans and pinto beans. Put the beans, cumin, garlic powder, chili powder (if using), salt, and water in the skillet. Cook for 2 to 3 minutes, or until the beans have heated through. Stir in the cooked rice and salsa. Remove from the heat. Cover the skillet and let it sit for 5 minutes.

**Slice the avocados.**

Cut the avocados lengthwise around the seeds (ask an adult for help). Gently hold on to each side and twist until they separate. Be careful not to squeeze too hard, or you'll bruise the fruit. Slide the tip of a spoon underneath the seeds, then scoop out the seeds and throw them away. Turn the avocado halves facedown on your cutting board and peel away the skin. Cut the halves into thin slices.

**Fill and roll the burritos.**

Put your tortillas on a work surface (you may need to work with 2 or 3 at a time, depending on how much space you have). Spread an equal amount of the filling into the center of each tortilla, then top each with avocado slices and any other toppings you like. Roll each burrito by folding the sides to the center and the bottom edge up. Once rolled, place each burrito, seam-side down, on a plate so it doesn't unroll. »

FUN FACT: "Burrito" is actually the Spanish word for "little donkey." It's true! In Spanish, donkeys are called burros, and some people say the ends of burritos look sort of like a donkey's ears.

# Baked Enchilada Rice Casserole

PREP TIME: 15 MINUTES
COOK TIME: 50 MINUTES
SERVES: 6

2 bell peppers, any color

1 (15-ounce) can black beans

2 cups instant long-grain
    brown rice

½ teaspoon onion powder

½ teaspoon garlic powder

2 (10-ounce) cans mild or medium
    red enchilada sauce

1 cup water

Warm water, as needed

Optional toppings: Sliced
    avocado, vegan sour cream,
    chopped lettuce

## TOOLS/EQUIPMENT

- Cutting board
- Knife
- Can opener
- Colander
- 9-by-13-inch baking dish
- Aluminum foil
- Spoon
- Oven mitts or pot holders

**Prepare the ingredients.**

Preheat the oven to 375°F. Cut the bell peppers into large dice. Drain and rinse the black beans.

**Mix together the casserole.**

Put the bell peppers and beans in a 9-by-13-inch casserole dish. Stir in the rice, onion powder, garlic powder, enchilada sauce, and water to combine.

**Bake.**

Cover the baking dish with aluminum foil. Transfer it to the oven and bake for 30 minutes. Pull back the foil and stir, then re-cover and bake for 20 more minutes, or until the rice has fully cooked. Using oven mitts, remove the casserole from the oven. Let it sit for 5 minutes before serving. If the casserole is too dry, stir in 2 to 3 tablespoons of warm water. Serve with your favorite toppings.

> **TRY INSTEAD:** If you have veggies on hand, add them with the bell peppers and beans. Diced onion, squash, sweet potatoes, and even frozen corn would be delicious.

# Meatless Shepherd's Pie

**FOR THE MASHED POTATOES**

Nonstick cooking spray, for coating the baking dish

2 pounds Yukon Gold potatoes, all of similar size

3 tablespoons vegan butter

½ cup unsweetened nondairy milk

¼ teaspoon salt, plus more for seasoning

⅛ teaspoon freshly ground black pepper, plus more for seasoning

**FOR THE VEGGIE FILLING**

1 (15-ounce) can Great Northern beans

⅓ cup vegetable broth

1 (10-ounce) package frozen mixed vegetables

1 teaspoon Italian seasoning

¼ teaspoon garlic powder

Freshly ground black pepper

**Turn on the oven and prep your baking dish.**

Place a rack in the center of the oven and preheat the oven to 400°F. Lightly coat a 1½-quart baking dish with cooking spray.

**Boil and mash the potatoes.**

Quarter the potatoes and put them in a large pot. Add enough water to cover the potatoes by about 1 inch. Bring to a boil over high heat. Cook for 15 to 20 minutes, or until the potatoes are easily pierced with a fork. Remove from the heat. Place a colander in the sink and drain the potatoes in it. Return them to the pot. Add the butter, milk, salt, and pepper. Using a potato masher, mash the potatoes completely. Taste, adding more salt and pepper as needed.

**Make the vegetable filling.**

While the potatoes cook, drain and rinse the Great Northern beans. Pour the vegetable broth into a medium pot. Bring to a boil over medium-high heat. Add the beans, frozen vegetables, Italian seasoning, and garlic powder. Reduce the heat to low. Simmer for 10 to 12 minutes, or until most of the broth has evaporated. Remove from the heat.

- 1½-quart baking dish
- Cutting board
- Knife
- 2 pots: 1 large, 1 medium
- Fork
- Colander
- Measuring cups and spoons
- Potato masher
- Can opener
- Rubber/silicone spatula
- Oven mitts or pot holders

**Assemble and bake.**

Mix ½ cup of the mashed potatoes into the vegetable mixture, then transfer them to the baking dish. Top with the remaining mashed potatoes, using a rubber spatula to spread it smoothly. Season with a sprinkle of pepper. Place the dish on the center rack in the oven and bake for 15 minutes, or until heated through. Using oven mitts, remove the pie from the oven.

> TRY INSTEAD: Make the casserole with sweet potatoes instead of Yukon Golds.

Veggie Potpie

# Veggie Potpie

**PREP TIME:** 20 MINUTES
**COOK TIME:** 30 MINUTES
**SERVES:** 6

Nonstick cooking spray, for
   coating the baking dish
3 red potatoes
1 bell pepper, any color
2 large carrots
2 celery stalks
1 cup frozen peas
2 tablespoons vegan butter
½ teaspoon salt
½ teaspoon onion powder
⅛ teaspoon freshly ground
   black pepper
¼ cup whole-wheat flour
1½ cups vegetable broth
½ cup unsweetened nondairy milk
1 sheet puff pastry, thawed
   and unrolled

**TOOLS/EQUIPMENT**

- 8-by-8-inch baking dish
- Cutting board
- Knife
- Large skillet or pot with lid
- Measuring cups and spoons
- Wooden spoon or
  rubber/silicone spatula
- Oven mitts or pot holders

**Turn on the oven and prep your baking dish.**
Preheat the oven to 375°F. Coat an 8-by-8-inch
baking dish with cooking spray.

**Chop the veggies.**
Cut the potatoes and bell pepper into a ½-inch
dice. Cut the carrots into circles and the celery
into half-moons. Take the peas out of the freezer.

**Cook the veggies.**
In a large skillet, melt the butter over medium-low
heat. Add the potatoes, bell pepper, carrots, and
celery. Stir in the salt, onion powder, and black
pepper. Cover the skillet and cook, stirring occasionally, for 5 minutes.

**Thicken it up.**
Stir in the flour, combining it as best you can.
Cook for 1 to 2 minutes. Pour in the vegetable
broth and milk, stirring until the flour lumps are
gone. Increase the heat to medium. Simmer for
4 to 5 minutes, or until the mixture thickens. Stir
in the frozen peas. Remove from the heat. »

**Top the pie and bake.**

Carefully pour the vegetable mixture into the prepared baking dish. Cover the top with the puff pastry, trimming it as needed so no more than ¼ inch of dough hangs over the edges of the baking dish. Cut 3 or 4 slits in the top to allow the steam from the hot veggies to escape, which prevents your puff pastry from getting too soggy. Transfer the dish to the oven and bake for 15 minutes, or until the crust is a nice golden brown. Using oven mitts, remove the potpie from the oven. Let cool for at least 5 minutes before serving.

FUN FACT: Not all premade puff pastries are vegan, but many are. Pepperidge Farm brand is what I call "accidentally vegan," which means it's not marketed as vegan, even though it is. It is available at most stores and is the brand I use.

# Barbecue Sweet Potatoes with Jasmine Rice

PREP TIME: 15 MINUTES
COOK TIME: 1 HOUR 5 MINUTES
SERVES: 4

1 cup jasmine rice
1¼ cups water
1 cup vegetable broth
2 teaspoons cornstarch
2 tablespoons tomato paste
2 tablespoons maple syrup
2 tablespoons soy sauce
1 teaspoon olive oil
1 teaspoon smoked paprika
½ teaspoon garlic powder
¼ teaspoon chili powder
2 medium or large sweet potatoes
Salt

TOOLS/EQUIPMENT

- Medium saucepan with lid
- Medium mixing bowl
- Whisk
- Peeler
- Cutting board
- Knife
- 7-by-11-inch baking dish
- Aluminum foil
- Oven mitts or pot holders

**Make the rice.**

In a medium saucepan, combine the rice and water. Bring to a boil over high heat. Reduce the heat to low. Cover the saucepan and simmer for 12 minutes, or until the water has been absorbed. Remove from the heat. Keep covered for 10 minutes, then fluff with a fork.

**Mix the barbecue sauce.**

Meanwhile, preheat the oven to 400°F. In a medium mixing bowl, whisk together the vegetable broth and cornstarch until the cornstarch has dissolved. Whisk in the tomato paste, maple syrup, soy sauce, olive oil, smoked paprika, garlic powder, and chili powder.

**Prep the sweet potatoes.**

Peel the sweet potatoes, then cut into ¾-inch pieces. Put them in a 7-by-11-inch baking dish, then pour the sauce over the top. Stir, then cover with aluminum foil.

**Bake.**

Transfer the baking dish to the oven. Bake for 25 minutes, then remove and discard the foil. Stir well, then bake for 25 more minutes, or until the sweet potatoes are tender and the sauce is nice and thick. Using oven mitts, remove them from the oven. »

**Serve.**

Taste the sauce and add salt as needed. Serve the sweet potatoes over rice.

TROUBLESHOOTING: Rice can be tough to get right the first time you make it, but the trick is to leave the cover on the entire time it's cooking, even though it can be tempting to peek! When the cooking time is up and you need to check to see if the liquid has been absorbed, do it as quickly as you can.

# Sloppy Joe Casserole

**PREP TIME:** 20 MINUTES

**COOK TIME:** 40 MINUTES

**SERVES:** 6

Nonstick cooking spray, for coating the baking dish

1 green bell pepper

1 roma tomato

1 (15-ounce) can kidney beans

12 pickle chips

2 (8-count) tubes crescent roll dough (Pillsbury and many store brands are vegan; double-check the label)

4 tablespoons water, divided, plus more as needed

½ teaspoon onion powder

1 (15-ounce) can vegetarian refried beans

¼ cup quick-cooking oats

2 tablespoons spicy brown mustard

¼ teaspoon chili powder (optional)

**TOOLS/EQUIPMENT**

- 2-quart baking dish
- Cutting board
- Knife
- Can opener
- Colander
- Nonstick skillet
- Oven mitts or pot holders

**Turn on the oven and prep your baking dish.**

Preheat the oven to 350°F. Lightly coat a 2-quart baking dish with cooking spray.

**Chop the veggies.**

Dice the green bell pepper and tomato. Drain and rinse the kidney beans. Quarter the pickle chips.

**Shape the crescent rolls.**

Open the tubes of crescent rolls and roll them into their crescent shape, starting with the wider end of the triangle and rolling toward the narrow end. (I like to lay them out on a piece of parchment paper or aluminum foil.)

**Make the sloppy Joe mixture.**

In a nonstick skillet, heat 2 tablespoons water over medium heat. Add the green bell pepper and onion powder. Cook for 2 to 3 minutes, or until the bell pepper just starts to soften. Add another tablespoon of water if the skillet gets dry. Stir in the tomato, kidney beans, pickles, refried beans, oats, mustard, chili powder (if using), and remaining 2 tablespoons of water. Increase the heat to medium-high. Simmer, stirring often, for about 5 minutes. You want it nice and hot without burning it on the bottom. Remove from the heat. »

**Assemble and bake the casserole.**

Spoon the sloppy Joe mixture into the prepared baking dish. Top with the crescent rolls, creating one nearly solid layer of doughy crescents. You may have to curve them a bit to fit. Transfer the dish to the oven and bake for 20 to 30 minutes, or until the crescent rolls have cooked through. You can lift the edge of one to check underneath (ask an adult for help). Using oven mitts, remove the casserole from the oven. Let cool for 5 to 10 minutes before serving.

> TROUBLESHOOTING: All ovens are different, so don't worry if the casserole takes a little longer than 30 minutes to bake in your oven.

Baked Chickpea Burgers

# Baked Chickpea Burgers

**PREP TIME:** 10 MINUTES, PLUS 20 MINUTES TO CHILL
**COOK TIME:** 25 MINUTES
**SERVES:** 4

1 tablespoon chia seeds
2½ tablespoons water
1 (15-ounce) can chickpeas
½ bell pepper, any color
1 large carrot
1 teaspoon ground cumin
½ teaspoon salt
¼ teaspoon onion powder
¼ teaspoon freshly ground
  black pepper
½ cup bread crumbs
Nonstick cooking spray, for
  coating the baking sheet
4 whole-wheat burger buns
Optional toppings: Lettuce,
  pickles, sliced tomato, ketchup,
  vegan mayonnaise

**TOOLS/EQUIPMENT**

- Mixing bowls: 1 small, 1 medium
- Measuring cups and spoons
- Spoon
- Can opener
- Colander
- Cutting board
- Knife
- Food processor
- Rubber/silicone spatula
- Large rimmed baking sheet
- Oven mitts or pot holders

**Mix your chia "egg."**
In a small mixing bowl, stir together the chia seeds and water. This creates an egg substitute called a "chia egg."

**Prepare the chickpeas and veggies.**
Drain and rinse the chickpeas. Chop the bell pepper and carrot into large chunks.

**Blend.**
Put the bell pepper and carrot in a food processor. Pulse just until chopped into small chickpea-size pieces. Add the chickpeas and process on low speed for 5 to 10 seconds. A few whole chickpeas are fine, but you want the majority to be blended—just not until it looks creamy, like hummus.

**Finish the burger mixture and chill.**
Using a rubber spatula, scrape the chickpea mixture into a medium mixing bowl. Add the cumin, salt, onion powder, black pepper, bread crumbs, and chia egg. Stir until well mixed. Cover the bowl and refrigerate for 20 minutes.

**Turn on the oven and prep your baking sheet.**
Preheat the oven to 375°F. Lightly coat a large rimmed baking sheet with cooking spray. »

**Cook the burgers.**

Form the burger mixture into 4 equal patties. Put them on the prepared baking sheet. Transfer it to the oven and bake for 12 minutes. Flip the patties and bake for 8 to 10 minutes, or until lightly golden. Using oven mitts, remove the burgers from the oven. Serve on the buns with your favorite toppings.

 TRY INSTEAD: Like a little heat? Add ½ teaspoon your favorite hot sauce in step 4!

# Sweet 'n' Sour Tofu

**PREP TIME:** 20 MINUTES
**COOK TIME:** 45 TO 50 MINUTES
**SERVES:** 4

Nonstick cooking spray,
    for coating
1 (14-ounce) block firm tofu, well
    pressed (see page 23)
½ sweet onion
1 green bell pepper
2 medium to large carrots
1 (8-ounce) can sliced
    water chestnuts
2 tablespoons water, plus more
    as needed
¾ cup jarred sweet and sour
    sauce, plus more as needed
2 cups cooked brown rice (either
    prepared in advance or
    microwavable, like Uncle Ben's)

**TOOLS/EQUIPMENT**

- Clean kitchen towels or tofu press
- Cutting board(s)
- Baking sheet
- Aluminum foil
- Knife
- Oven mitts or pot holders
- Tongs
- Can opener
- Colander
- Large skillet
- Rubber/silicone spatula

**Turn on the oven and prep your baking sheet.**
Preheat the oven to 420°F. Line a baking sheet with aluminum foil and lightly coat it with cooking spray.

**Bake the tofu.**
Cut the tofu into bite-size cubes and place them in a single layer on the prepared baking sheet. Transfer the tofu to the oven and bake for 20 minutes. Using oven mitts, remove the tofu from the oven. Spritz the top of the tofu cubes with cooking spray. Using tongs, flip the cubes. Using oven mitts again, return the baking sheet to the oven and bake for 10 to 15 minutes, or until the tofu is lightly golden brown and slightly puffy. Using oven mitts again, remove the tofu from the oven.

**Prepare the veggies.**
Cut the onion and green bell pepper into bite-size chunks. Cut the carrots into thin circles (or half circles if the carrots are thick). Drain the water chestnuts.

**Cook the veggies and tofu.**

In a large skillet, heat the water over medium-low heat. Add the onion, green bell pepper, and carrots. Sauté, stirring, for 4 to 5 minutes, or until just softened. Add another tablespoon of water if the skillet gets dry. Add the tofu, sweet and sour sauce, and water chestnuts. Simmer for 4 to 5 minutes, or until everything is warmed through. Depending on the sauce you use, you may need to add another ¼ cup or so. You want it saucy, but not soupy. Remove from the heat. Serve over cooked brown rice.

> TRY INSTEAD: This dish is perfect for adding more veggies . . . and even fruit! Pineapple chunks (canned in juice, not syrup, are the healthiest and most delicious), snap peas, celery—whatever your favorite is!

# Spaghetti and Beanballs

**PREP TIME:** 15 MINUTES
**COOK TIME:** 40 MINUTES
**SERVES:** 4

FOR THE BEANBALLS

Nonstick cooking spray,
    for coating
1 (15-ounce) can kidney beans
¼ cup bread crumbs
2 teaspoons olive oil
2 teaspoons Italian seasoning
½ teaspoon onion powder
¼ teaspoon freshly squeezed
    lemon juice
¼ teaspoon salt
¼ teaspoon red pepper
    flakes (optional)
2 teaspoons water (optional)

FOR THE SPAGHETTI

4 to 6 quarts water
Pinch salt
8 ounces dried spaghetti or
    angel hair
1 (24-ounce) jar your favorite
    pasta sauce
Fresh basil, for topping (optional)

**Turn on the oven and prep your baking sheet.**
Preheat the oven to 375°F. Coat a large rimmed
baking sheet with cooking spray.

**Mash the beans and add seasonings.**
Drain and rinse the kidney beans. Pour them into
a large mixing bowl and mash using a potato
masher or the back of a fork. Make sure most of
the beans are mashed (although some bigger
pieces are okay). Add the bread crumbs, olive oil,
Italian seasoning, onion powder, lemon juice, salt,
and red pepper flakes (if using). Using your clean
hands, mix everything to combine.

**Roll the beanballs.**
Still using your hands, roll the bean mixture into
12 identical balls, making sure you squeeze them
tight and round. If the mixture isn't sticking
together, add the water, 1 teaspoon at a time, and
mix it in, then try again.

**Bake the beanballs.**
Place the beanballs at least 1 inch apart on the
prepared baking sheet. Give them a light spritz
with cooking spray. Transfer the beanballs to
the oven and bake for 20 minutes. Using tongs,
turn the beanballs over, spritz again with cooking spray, and bake for 15 to 20 minutes, or
until they're nice and golden. Using oven mitts,
remove the beanballs from the oven. »

TOOLS/EQUIPMENT

- Large rimmed baking sheet
- Can opener
- Colander
- Large mixing bowl
- Potato masher or fork
- Measuring cups and spoons
- Tongs
- Oven mitts or pot holders
- Large pot with lid
- Pasta spoon

**Cook the spaghetti.**

While the beanballs bake, in a large pot, bring the water to a rolling boil over high heat. Add the salt, then the spaghetti. Using a pasta spoon, stir gently until the spaghetti softens enough that it is covered by the water. Return to a boil and cook for 9 to 10 minutes for spaghetti, or 4 to 5 minutes for angel hair. Stir gently every couple of minutes. When you think the pasta is done, use the pasta spoon to pull out one strand. Let it cool for a few moments, then bite into it to make sure it's done. If it's crunchy, it isn't done and needs to cook longer. Check again in another minute. If it's slightly firm or just barely soft, it is done! Remove from the heat. Place a colander in the sink and drain the spaghetti in it (ask an adult for help and watch out for the hot steam). Return the spaghetti to the pot.

**Combine the spaghetti, sauce, and beanballs.**

Stir in the pasta sauce. Add the beanballs and gently stir so they don't break apart too much. Cover the pot and let sit for 5 minutes. Using your pasta spoon or tongs, scoop the spaghetti into bowls and top with basil (if using).

PRO TIP: To make this recipe gluten-free, use gluten-free panko bread crumbs in the beanballs and gluten-free pasta.

# Korean-Inspired Barbecue Bowls

**PREP TIME:** 15 MINUTES
**COOK TIME:** 35 MINUTES
**SERVES:** 4

Nonstick cooking spray, for coating
1 (14-ounce) block firm tofu, well
    pressed (see page 23)
1 red bell pepper
2 tablespoons water, plus more
    as needed
4 rounded cups broccoli florets
¾ cup bottled Korean
    barbecue sauce
2 cups cooked brown rice (either
    prepared in advance or
    microwavable, like Uncle Ben's)

**TOOLS/EQUIPMENT**

- Clean kitchen towels or tofu press
- Cutting board(s)
- Baking sheet
- Aluminum foil
- Knife
- Oven mitts or pot holders
- Tongs
- Measuring cups and spoons
- Large skillet with lid

**Turn on the oven and prep your baking sheet.**
Preheat the oven to 420°F. Line a baking sheet with aluminum foil and lightly coat it with cooking spray.

**Bake the tofu.**
Cut the tofu into bite-size cubes. Place in a single layer on the prepared baking sheet. Bake for 20 minutes. Using oven mitts, remove the tofu from the oven. Spritz the top of the tofu cubes with cooking spray. Using tongs, flip the cubes. Using oven mitts again, return the baking sheet to the oven and bake for 10 to 15 minutes, or until the tofu is lightly golden brown and slightly puffy. Using oven mitts again, remove the tofu from the oven.

**Cook the veggies.**
Cut the red bell pepper into large dice (about ½ inch). In a large skillet, heat the water over medium-low heat. Add the red bell pepper and broccoli. Cover the skillet and simmer, stirring occasionally, for 2 to 3 minutes, adding another tablespoon of water if the skillet dries out.

**Add the flavor.**
Stir in the tofu and barbecue sauce. Simmer uncovered for 5 minutes. Remove from the heat. Serve over the rice.

HELPFUL HINT: Most grocery stores carry premade Korean barbecue sauce in their international aisle.

# "Cheesy" Cauliflower

**PREP TIME:** 15 MINUTES
**COOK TIME:** 25 MINUTES
**SERVES:** 4

1 large russet potato
2 carrots
1 cup unsweetened nondairy milk
½ cup nutritional yeast
2 tablespoons olive oil
2 teaspoons freshly squeezed
   lemon juice
1 teaspoon yellow mustard
1 teaspoon vegan
   Worcestershire sauce
1 teaspoon salt, plus more
   for seasoning
1 teaspoon garlic powder
1 teaspoon onion powder
¼ teaspoon freshly ground
   black pepper
2 (16-ounce) bags frozen
   cauliflower florets

**TOOLS/EQUIPMENT**
- Peeler
- Cutting board
- Knife
- Medium saucepan
- Colander
- Measuring cups and spoons
- Blender
- Rubber spatula

**Cook the potato and carrots.**

Peel the potato and cut into ¾-inch pieces. Peel the carrots and cut into ½-inch pieces. Put them in a medium saucepan and add enough water to cover them. Bring to a boil. Cook for 8 to 10 minutes, or until fork-tender. Remove from the heat. Place a colander in the sink and drain the vegetables in it.

**Make the "cheese" sauce.**

Put the cooked potato and carrots, milk, nutritional yeast, olive oil, lemon juice, mustard, vegan Worcestershire sauce, salt, garlic powder, onion powder, and pepper in a blender. Blend on high speed until smooth. If the sauce is sticking to the sides, pause and use a rubber spatula to scrape down the sides. Taste, adding more salt as needed.

**Cook the cauliflower.**

Put the frozen cauliflower in the saucepan and cook according to the package instructions, minus 1 minute. Remove from the heat. Drain the cauliflower and return to the pan. »

**Combine the "cheese" and cauliflower.**

Pour about three-fourths of the cheese sauce over the cauliflower in the pan. Stir until the cauliflower is covered. Cook over medium-low heat, stirring occasionally, for 4 to 5 minutes, or until heated through. Remove from the heat.

HELPFUL HINT: Reheated leftovers sometimes get dried out, so keep the extra cheese sauce on the side to add to leftovers. This recipe makes 4 servings as a main dish, 6 as a side.

# Spicy Peanut Noodles

PREP TIME: 15 MINUTES
COOK TIME: 20 MINUTES
SERVES: 4

## FOR THE SAUCE

½ cup creamy peanut butter
2 tablespoons rice vinegar
1 tablespoon gluten-free
  low-sodium soy sauce
1 teaspoon chili sauce (like
  sriracha), plus more
  for seasoning
¼ teaspoon ground ginger
Juice of ½ lime
¼ cup hot water

## FOR THE NOODLES

2 tablespoons water, plus more for
  cooking the noodles
8 ounces rice noodles
1 red bell pepper
½ cucumber
1 large carrot
¼ cup roasted chopped
  peanuts (optional)
¼ cup sliced scallions, green and
  white parts (optional)
½ lime, cut into wedges

**Make the sauce.**

In a small mixing bowl, whisk together the peanut butter, vinegar, soy sauce, chili sauce, ginger, lime juice, and hot water until smooth. Taste, adding more chili sauce if desired.

**Cook the rice noodles.**

Bring a large pot of water to a boil over high heat. Add the rice noodles and cook according to the package instructions (they generally need to be boiled for 4 to 6 minutes), or until tender but still firm. Remove from the heat. Place a colander in the sink and drain the noodles in it. Rinse the noodles well with cold water.

**Prep your veggies.**

Cut the red bell pepper into thin strips about 1 inch long. Halve the cucumber lengthwise, then cut it into thin half-moons. Cut the carrot into thin circles (or half circles, if it's thick).

**Finish the veggies and noodles.**

In a large skillet, heat the water over medium heat. Add the red bell pepper, cucumber, and carrot. Sauté for 2 to 3 minutes, then stir in the noodles and sauce. Reduce the heat to low. Cook, stirring occasionally, for 2 to 3 minutes. Remove from the heat. Top with peanuts (if using) and scallions (if using) and serve with lime wedges on the side for squeezing.

- Small mixing bowl
- Measuring cups and spoons
- Whisk
- Large pot
- Colander
- Cutting board
- Knife
- Large skillet
- Rubber/silicone spatula

TRY INSTEAD: Want to feed a couple of extra people with this recipe? Add baked tofu, using the instructions from Korean-Inspired Barbecue Bowls on page 109.

Coconut Curry Bowls

# Coconut Curry Bowls

PREP TIME: 15 MINUTES
COOK TIME: 15 MINUTES
SERVES: 4

2 large carrots
1 (15-ounce) can Great
    Northern beans
¼ cup water, plus 2 teaspoons,
    divided, plus more as needed
3 heaping cups broccoli florets
1 (15-ounce) can light coconut milk
2 teaspoons red curry paste
½ teaspoon salt
2 teaspoons cornstarch
4 cups frozen cauliflower rice

TOOLS/EQUIPMENT

- Cutting board
- Knife
- Can opener
- Colander
- Large skillet
- Spoon
- Small mixing bowl
- Small whisk

**Prep the ingredients.**
Cut the carrots into thin circles. Drain and rinse the Great Northern beans.

**Cook the veggies.**
In a large skillet, heat ¼ cup water over medium-low heat. Add the carrots and broccoli. Simmer, stirring occasionally, for 3 to 4 minutes, adding another tablespoon of water if the skillet gets dry.

**Combine the flavors.**
Stir in the beans, coconut milk, red curry paste, and salt. In a small mixing bowl, whisk together the cornstarch and remaining 2 teaspoons of water, then add this slurry to the skillet. Increase the heat to high. Once boiling, reduce the heat to low. Simmer for about 5 minutes, or until the sauce thickens and the veggies are tender. Remove from the heat.

**Prepare the cauliflower rice.**
While the curry simmers, cook the cauliflower rice according to the package instructions. (Some brands differ, but many are in microwavable bags and only take a couple minutes to cook.) Divide the rice among 4 bowls and top with the curry.

DID YOU KNOW? There are many different flavors and even colors of curries out there from many different parts of the world. This version is simple and mild and a great place to start before experimenting on your own.

Cookies 'n' Cream Cake (page 130)

7

# Desserts & Treats

Baked Cinnamon-Sugar Donuts

# Baked Cinnamon-Sugar Donuts

**PREP TIME:** 25 MINUTES
**COOK TIME:** 20 MINUTES
**SERVES:** 6
(MAKES 12 DONUTS)

### FOR THE DONUTS

Nonstick cooking spray, for coating the donut trays
1½ cups all-purpose flour
½ cup granulated sugar
¼ cup packed light brown sugar
2 teaspoons baking powder
½ teaspoon ground cinnamon
¼ teaspoon salt
¾ cup unsweetened nondairy milk
5 tablespoons melted coconut oil
2 tablespoons unsweetened applesauce
1½ teaspoons vanilla extract

### FOR THE TOPPING

2 tablespoons vegan butter
½ cup granulated sugar
1 teaspoon ground cinnamon

### TOOLS/EQUIPMENT

- 2 (6-count) donut trays or 2 (6-cup) muffin tins
- Large mixing bowl, preferably a batter bowl with a spout for pouring
- Measuring cups and spoons
- Whisk
- Large spoon
- Oven mitts or pot holders
- Wire rack
- 2 wide, shallow bowls (1 microwave-safe)

**Turn on the oven and prep your donut trays.**
Preheat the oven to 350°F. Lightly coat 2 (6-count) donut trays with cooking spray.

**Mix the batter.**
In a large mixing bowl, whisk together the flour, granulated sugar, brown sugar, baking powder, cinnamon, and salt. Add the milk, melted coconut oil, applesauce, and vanilla. Whisk well to combine and break up any lumps.

**Pour the batter into the trays and bake.**
If you are using a mixing bowl with a spout, carefully pour the batter into the prepared trays. If not, use a large spoon to fill the trays with batter. (Ask an adult for help if needed.) Bake for 14 to 15 minutes, or until the donuts are light golden brown on top. Using oven mitts, remove the donuts from the oven.

**Let cool.**
Let the donuts cool in the trays for a few minutes, then transfer the donuts to a wire rack to cool completely.

**Prepare the cinnamon-sugar topping.**
In a wide, shallow, microwave-safe bowl, melt the butter in the microwave on high power, just a few seconds at a time, stirring between each cooking time. Ask an adult for help with this. In a second wide, shallow bowl, stir together the granulated sugar and cinnamon. »

**Decorate the donuts.**

Holding each donut upside down, just barely dip it into the melted butter for just a second, then dip it into the cinnamon sugar. Repeat for each donut. Line the donuts up on a tray and sprinkle the remaining cinnamon sugar over the tops.

TRY INSTEAD: Try these donuts with a vanilla glaze instead of cinnamon sugar! Skip steps 5 and 6 and then to make the glaze, in a medium bowl, whisk together 1½ cups powdered sugar, 2 tablespoons non-dairy milk, and 1½ teaspoons vanilla extract until smooth. Hold each donut upside down and dip into the glaze, then let rest until the glaze hardens.

# Spiced Vanilla Pudding

**PREP TIME:** 5 MINUTES, PLUS 2 HOURS TO CHILL
**COOK TIME:** 10 MINUTES
**SERVES:** 4

⅓ cup sugar
¼ cup cornstarch
¼ teaspoon salt
2 cups unsweetened nondairy milk
1 teaspoon vanilla extract
⅛ teaspoon ground nutmeg

TOOLS/EQUIPMENT

- Small or medium saucepan or pot
- Measuring cups and spoons
- Whisk
- Rubber/silicone spatula
- Medium mixing bowl
- Plastic wrap

**Mix the dry ingredients.**
In a small saucepan, whisk together the sugar, cornstarch, and salt to combine.

**Add the milk and begin to cook.**
Pour in the milk and whisk until completely blended. Cook over medium-low heat, stirring constantly, for 2 to 3 minutes, or just until you start to see a bit of steam rising. Reduce the heat to low.

**Continue to cook.**
Switch to a rubber spatula and cook, stirring constantly, for 2 to 3 minutes, or until the pudding thickens. The spatula will help ensure nothing is stuck to the sides or bottom of the pan.

**Add the final seasonings and chill.**
Remove the pan from heat. Stir in the vanilla and nutmeg. Let cool for 8 to 10 minutes, stirring occasionally. Pour the pudding into a medium mixing bowl and place a layer of plastic wrap directly on the top of the pudding. (When the pudding is exposed to air in the refrigerator, the very top will form a thin layer that is a different texture. It's edible but nicer without it. The plastic wrap will help keep this "skin" from forming.) Refrigerate for 2 hours, or until completely firm.

PRO TIP: Serve topped with 1 to 2 cups fresh blueberries and sliced strawberries to make this dessert extra special.

Peanut Butter–Coconut Cookies

# Peanut Butter–Coconut Cookies

**PREP TIME:** 20 MINUTES, PLUS 15 MINUTES TO COOL

**COOK TIME:** 15 MINUTES

**SERVES:** 10
(MAKES 20 COOKIES)

1½ cups all-purpose flour

¼ cup unsweetened shredded coconut

1 teaspoon baking powder

1 teaspoon baking soda

8 tablespoons (1 stick) vegan butter, at room temperature

½ cup granulated sugar

½ cup packed light brown sugar

1 cup creamy peanut butter

1 tablespoon vanilla extract

1 tablespoon unsweetened nondairy milk, plus more as needed (optional; depending on the peanut butter you use, this may not be necessary)

## TOOLS/EQUIPMENT

- Baking sheet
- Parchment paper
- Small mixing bowl
- Measuring cups and spoons
- Spoon
- Stand mixer with paddle attachment, or large mixing bowl and handheld electric mixer
- Fork
- Oven mitts or pot holders
- Flat turning spatula
- Wire rack

**Turn on the oven and prep your baking sheet.**
Preheat the oven to 375°F. Line a baking sheet with parchment paper.

**Combine the dry ingredients.**
In a small mixing bowl, stir together the flour, coconut, baking powder, and baking soda.

**Combine the wet ingredients.**
In the bowl of a stand mixer, combine the butter, granulated sugar, and light brown sugar. Cream together on medium speed for 2 to 3 minutes. Add the peanut butter and vanilla. Mix just until combined. Turn off the mixer. Slowly add the dry ingredients to the wet ingredients, stirring by hand until well mixed.

**Check your dough.**
Try rolling 1 tablespoon of the dough into a ball. If it sticks together, your dough is ready. If it's dry and crumbly, stir in 1 tablespoon nondairy milk, then try again. Repeat until you're able to roll a mostly smooth ball of dough. »

**Shape and bake the cookies.**
Using a tablespoon, portion the cookie dough. Using your clean hands, roll each portion into a ball and place them evenly spaced apart on the prepared baking sheet. Using the back of a fork, flatten the cookies, creating a crisscross pattern. Transfer the baking sheet to the oven and bake for 10 to 14 minutes, or until the edges are set and the tops are golden brown. Using oven mitts, remove the cookies from the oven. Let the cookies cool on the baking sheet for 5 to 6 minutes, then using a turning spatula, move them to a wire rack to cool for 10 more minutes.

TROUBLESHOOTING: Wondering why you may or may not need to add milk to the dough? Some peanut butter brands have more moisture than others. By waiting to add the milk, you can prevent the dough from becoming too moist and then spreading too much during baking.

# Chocolate Chip Cookies

**PREP TIME:** 25 MINUTES
**COOK TIME:** 15 MINUTES
**SERVES:** 10
(MAKES 20 COOKIES)

8 tablespoons (1 stick) vegan
    butter, at room temperature
1 cup packed light brown sugar
¼ cup unsweetened nondairy milk
1 tablespoon vanilla extract
2 cups all-purpose flour
2 teaspoons cornstarch
1 teaspoon baking powder
1 teaspoon baking soda
¼ teaspoon ground cinnamon
¼ teaspoon salt
1 cup vegan chocolate chips

TOOLS/EQUIPMENT

- Large rimmed baking sheet
- Parchment paper
- Stand mixer with paddle
  attachment, or large mixing bowl
  and handheld electric mixer
- Measuring cups and spoons
- Small mixing bowl
- Whisk
- Rubber/silicone spatula
- Flat turning spatula
- Oven mitts or pot holders
- Wire rack

**Turn on the oven and prep your baking sheet.**
Preheat the oven to 350°F. Line a large rimmed baking sheet with parchment paper.

**Mix the wet ingredients.**
Put the butter and brown sugar in the bowl of a stand mixer. Cream together on medium speed for 2 to 3 minutes. Add the milk and vanilla. Mix just until smooth.

**Mix the dry ingredients.**
In a small mixing bowl, whisk together the flour, cornstarch, baking powder, baking soda, cinnamon, and salt until completely mixed.

**Combine.**
Using the paddle attachment, slowly add the dry ingredients to the wet ingredients and mix. (I like to use the paddle attachment since it keeps anything from sticking to the sides of the bowl.) Stir just until completely mixed. Turn off the mixer. Using a turning spatula, stir in the chocolate chips. »

**Shape and bake the cookies.**

Now you get to use your clean hands! In the bowl, divide the cookie dough in half, then into quarters. This will help make sure your cookies are the same size. Divide each quarter into 5 pieces (you'll have 20 dough pieces), then roll the dough into balls. Place the cookie balls evenly spaced apart on the prepared baking sheet. Transfer the sheet to the oven and bake for 13 to 15 minutes, or until the tops are slightly golden brown. Using oven mitts, remove the cookies from the oven. Let cool for 5 minutes, then transfer the cookies to a wire rack to cool completely.

TRY INSTEAD: Vegan chocolate chunks, which are larger than chips, are a fun way to change up these cookies. Or try vegan white chocolate chips or chunks.

PB & J Ice Cream Pie

# PB & J Ice Cream Pie

PREP TIME: 20 MINUTES, PLUS
2 HOURS TO FREEZE

SERVES: 6

1 quart no-sugar-added vegan
  vanilla ice cream
½ cup creamy peanut butter
1 (9-inch) vegan Graham cracker
  piecrust (such as Keebler)
½ cup raspberry preserves

TOOLS/EQUIPMENT
- Large mixing bowl
- Measuring cups
- Rubber/silicone spatula
- Handheld electric mixer
- Spoon
- Aluminum foil or plastic wrap

**Blend the ice cream and peanut butter.**
Let the ice cream sit on the counter for 5 to
10 minutes, or until softened enough to scoop out
of the container. In a large mixing bowl, combine the ice cream and peanut butter. Using a
handheld electric mixer, mix on low speed until
smooth. Turn off the mixer.

**Start layering the pie.**
Pour the ice cream mixture into the piecrust
and smooth the top using the back of a spoon.
Loosely cover the pie with aluminum foil or plastic wrap. Freeze for 1 hour, or until the pie is firm
enough to hold the preserves on top.

**Add the preserves.**
Pour the preserves on top of the pie. Using the
back of a spoon, gently spread the preserves into
an even layer. Re-cover the pie and freeze for at
least 1 hour, or until solid.

TROUBLESHOOTING: Because the ice
cream layer has peanut butter in it,
it will freeze harder than ice cream normally
does. This means you need to let the pie sit
out for about 5 minutes before you'll be able
to enjoy it.

# Cookies 'n' Cream Cake

**PREP TIME:** 25 MINUTES
**COOK TIME:** 45 MINUTES
**SERVES:** 8

Nonstick cooking spray, for coating the loaf pan
1½ cups all-purpose flour
½ cup granulated sugar
½ cup packed light brown sugar
¼ cup cocoa powder
1 teaspoon baking soda
½ teaspoon salt
1 cup unsweetened nondairy milk
⅓ cup unsweetened applesauce
1½ teaspoons vanilla extract
1 teaspoon apple cider vinegar
8 vegan chocolate sandwich cookies, like Newman-O's or Oreos
8 ounces whipped coconut topping, such as So Delicious Cocowhip

## TOOLS/EQUIPMENT

- 9-by-5-inch loaf pan
- Mixing bowls: 1 large, 1 medium
- Measuring cups and spoons
- Whisk
- Rubber/silicone spatula
- Oven mitts or pot holders
- Wire rack
- Cutting board
- Knife

**Turn on the oven and prep your cake pan.**
Place a rack in the center of the oven and preheat the oven to 350°F. Lightly coat the inside of a 9-by-5-inch loaf pan with cooking spray.

**Mix the dry ingredients.**
In a large mixing bowl, whisk together the flour, granulated sugar, brown sugar, cocoa powder, baking soda, and salt to combine well.

**Mix the wet ingredients, then combine to make the batter.**
In a medium mixing bowl, using a rubber spatula, stir together the milk, applesauce, vanilla, and apple cider vinegar. Slowly add the wet ingredients to the dry ingredients, stirring as you go.

**Bake.**
Pour the batter into the prepared pan. Place on the center rack in the oven and bake for 40 to 45 minutes, or until the sides of the cake have begun to pull away from the pan. (You can also stick a toothpick into the center of the cake; if it comes out clean, the cake is done!) Using oven mitts, remove the pan from the oven. Transfer to a wire rack and let the cake cool in the pan. If you need it to cool quickly, refrigerate it.

**Chop the cookies.**

Coarsely chop the cookies into quarters. They will break apart a bit, but that's okay because you're sprinkling them on top!

**Finish and serve.**

Slice the cooled cake. Spread the whipped topping evenly over the top and sprinkle evenly with the cookies.

PRO TIP: Try breaking the cake up into small pieces and freezing them in an airtight container, then mixing them with your favorite vegan ice cream!

# Apple Crisp

PREP TIME: 25 MINUTES
COOK TIME: 40 MINUTES
SERVES: 8

Nonstick cooking spray, for
   coating the baking dish
5 apples
3 tablespoons granulated sugar
1 teaspoon ground cinnamon
¼ teaspoon salt
⅛ teaspoon ground nutmeg
¾ cup old-fashioned oats
¾ cup all-purpose flour
½ cup packed light brown sugar
½ teaspoon vanilla extract
5 tablespoons vegan butter

TOOLS/EQUIPMENT

- 9-inch square baking dish
- Peeler
- Cutting board
- Knife
- Mixing bowls: 1 large, 1 medium
- Measuring cups and spoons
- Spoon
- Small microwave-safe bowl
- Oven mitts or pot holders

**Turn on the oven and prep your baking dish.**
Preheat the oven to 375°F. Lightly coat a 9-inch
square baking dish with cooking spray.

**Peel and slice the apples.**
Peel the apples, then cut each apple away from
the core: Hold the apple, stem-side up, on the
cutting board and cut off each side, leaving the
core. Cut the apples into thin slices, being careful
to keep the thickness of your slices the same.

**Mix the filling.**
In a large mixing bowl, stir together the apples,
granulated sugar, cinnamon, salt, and nutmeg,
stirring until the apple pieces are coated. Pour it
into the prepared baking dish.

**Mix the topping.**
In a medium mixing bowl, stir together the
oats, flour, brown sugar, and vanilla. In a small
microwave-safe bowl, melt the butter in the
microwave on high power, just a few seconds at
a time, stirring between each cooking time. (Ask
an adult for help with this.) Stir the melted butter
into the oat mixture until it's evenly moistened.

**Add the topping and bake.**

Spoon the topping in an even layer over the filling in the baking dish. Transfer it to the oven and bake for 35 to 40 minutes (asking an adult to rotate the dish once about halfway through baking time), or until the filling is bubbly and the top is golden brown. Using oven mitts, remove from the oven. Let cool before serving.

TRY INSTEAD: Try substituting a Bartlett or Bosc pear for 1 or 2 of the apples. This makes it especially fun when your family is enjoying the crisp and trying to figure out what that wonderful flavor is!

Salted Caramel Sundaes

# Salted Caramel Sundaes

PREP TIME: 10 MINUTES

COOK TIME: 1 HOUR, PLUS
1 HOUR AT ROOM TEMPERATURE
AND OVERNIGHT TO CHILL

SERVES: 4

**FOR THE CARAMEL SAUCE**

1 (13½-ounce) can full-fat
    coconut milk
⅓ cup real maple syrup
¼ cup packed light brown sugar
½ teaspoon vanilla extract
1 teaspoon sea salt

**FOR THE SUNDAES**

1 pint vegan vanilla ice cream
Optional toppings: Coconut
    whipped cream,
    sprinkles, cherries

**TOOLS/EQUIPMENT**

- Medium saucepan
- Can opener
- Measuring cups and spoons
- Rubber/silicone spatula

**Make the caramel sauce.**

In a medium saucepan, combine the coconut milk, maple syrup, and light brown sugar. Cook over high heat, stirring occasionally using a rubber spatula, until the mixture begins to boil. Then cook, stirring continuously, for about 3 minutes.

**Reduce the caramel.**

Reduce the heat to low. Simmer, stirring occasionally, for 45 to 50 minutes, or until the sauce has cooked down by about half and is nice and thick. Remove from the heat. Stir in the vanilla and let it sit at room temperature for 45 minutes to 1 hour to thicken. Stir in the salt, cover the pan, and refrigerate for at least 8 hours, but overnight is best. This allows the flavor to deepen and the sauce to thicken completely.

**Build the sundaes.**

Scoop the ice cream into 4 serving bowls and top with the cooled caramel sauce and any toppings you like.

> TRY INSTEAD: Try these sundaes with chocolate ice cream or any other flavor you like.

# MEASUREMENT CONVERSIONS

## Volume Equivalents (Liquid)

| US STANDARD | US STANDARD (OUNCES) | METRIC (APPROXIMATE) |
|---|---|---|
| 2 tablespoons | 1 fl. oz. | 30 mL |
| ¼ cup | 2 fl. oz. | 60 mL |
| ½ cup | 4 fl. oz. | 120 mL |
| 1 cup | 8 fl. oz. | 240 mL |
| 1½ cups | 12 fl. oz. | 355 mL |
| 2 cups or 1 pint | 16 fl. oz. | 475 mL |
| 4 cups or 1 quart | 32 fl. oz. | 1 L |
| 1 gallon | 128 fl. oz. | 4 L |

## Oven Temperatures

| FAHRENHEIT (F) | CELSIUS (C) (APPROXIMATE) |
|---|---|
| 250°F | 120°C |
| 300°F | 150°C |
| 325°F | 165°C |
| 350°F | 180°C |
| 375°F | 190°C |
| 400°F | 200°C |
| 425°F | 220°C |
| 450°F | 230°C |

## Volume Equivalents (Dry)

| US STANDARD | METRIC (APPROXIMATE) |
|---|---|
| ⅛ teaspoon | 0.5 mL |
| ¼ teaspoon | 1 mL |
| ½ teaspoon | 2 mL |
| ¾ teaspoon | 4 mL |
| 1 teaspoon | 5 mL |
| 1 tablespoon | 15 mL |
| ¼ cup | 59 mL |
| ⅓ cup | 79 mL |
| ½ cup | 118 mL |
| ⅔ cup | 156 mL |
| ¾ cup | 177 mL |
| 1 cup | 235 mL |
| 2 cups or 1 pint | 475 mL |
| 3 cups | 700 mL |
| 4 cups or 1 quart | 1 L |

## Weight Equivalents

| US STANDARD | METRIC (APPROXIMATE) |
|---|---|
| ½ ounce | 15 g |
| 1 ounce | 30 g |
| 2 ounces | 60 g |
| 4 ounces | 115 g |
| 8 ounces | 225 g |
| 12 ounces | 340 g |
| 16 ounces or 1 pound | 455 g |

# RECIPE INDEX

# INDEX

# ABOUT THE AUTHOR

**Barb Musick** lives in Colorado with her ever-growing pack of rescue animals. She shares her adventures and love of food, travel, and animals on her blog, *That Was Vegan?*, along with vegan recipes everyone will love. She is the author of five cookbooks, including *The Complete Vegan Instant Pot Cookbook* and *Easy Vegan Comfort Food*. Visit her at ThatWasVegan.com.

CPSIA information can be obtained
at www.ICGtesting.com
Printed in the USA
JSHW041502061122
32696JS00002B/3